THE FAMILY Handyman

ULTIMATE
ORGANIZING
SOLUTIONS

KITCHEN

BATH

CLOSET

GARAGE

Reader's digest | The Reader's Digest Association Inc.
New York, NY/Montreal

Editorial and Production Team

Vern Johnson, Peggy McDermott, Rick Muscoplat, Mary Schwender, Marcia Roepke

Photography and Illustrations

Ron Chamberlain, Tom Fenenga, Bruce Kieffer, Mike Krivit, Don Mannes, Ramon Moreno, Shawn Nielsen, Doug Oudekerk, Frank Rohrbach III, Eugene Thompson, Bill Zuehlke

Text, photography and illustrations for *Ultimate Organizing Solutions* are based on articles previously published in *The Family Handyman* magazine (2915 Commers Dr., Suite 700, Eagan, MN 55121, familyhandyman.com). For information on advertising in *The Family Handyman* magazine, call (646) 293-6150.

ISBN: 978-1-62145-240-9

THE FAMILY HANDYMAN

Editor in Chief   Ken Collier
Project Editor   Eric Smith
Design & Layout   Diana Boger, Teresa Marrone, Bruce Bohnenstingl
Senior Editors   Travis Larson, Gary Wentz
Associate Editor   Jeff Gorton
Administrative Manager   Alice Garrett
Senior Copy Editor   Donna Bierbach
VP, Group Publisher   Russell S. Ellis

Published by Home Service Publications, Inc., a subsidiary of The Reader's Digest Association, Inc.

PRINTED IN CHINA

1 2 3 4 5 6 7 8 9 10

A NOTE TO OUR READERS: All do-it-yourself activities involve a degree of risk. Skills, materials, tools and site conditions vary widely. Although the editors have made every effort to ensure accuracy, the reader remains responsible for the selection and use of tools, materials and methods. Always obey local codes and laws, follow manufacturer instructions and observe safety precautions.

Contents

CHAPTER 4

Garage & basement

 CHAPTER 5

Outdoor organization & storage

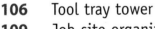

CHAPTER 6

Tools & materials

CHAPTER 7

Shelves & bookcases

1
Kitchen &
bathroom

Kitchen cabinet rollouts

Base cabinets have the least convenient storage space in the entire kitchen. Rollouts solve that problem. They make organizing and accessing your cabinet contents back-friendly and frustration-free.

If you're stuck with cabinets without rollouts, don't despair. Here you'll learn how to retrofit nearly any base cabinet with rollouts that'll work as well as or better than any factory-built units.

It's really very easy. Once you take measurements, you can build the rollout drawer (Photos 2–6), its "carrier" (Photos 7–9), and attach the drawer slides (Photos 6 and 7), all in

your shop. Mounting the unit in the cabinet is simple (Photos 10–12). You'll also learn how to construct a special rollout for recycling or trash (Photos 14–15).

The project will go faster if you have a table saw and miter saw to cut out all the pieces. A circular saw and cutting guide will work too; it'll just take a little longer. You can build a pair of rollouts in a Saturday morning.

WHAT IT TAKES

Time: 4 hours
Skill level: Intermediate

What wood products to buy

These rollout drawers are made entirely of 1/2-in. Baltic birch plywood. Baltic birch is favored by cabinetmakers because it's "void free," meaning that the thin veneers of the plywood core are solid wood. Therefore sanded edges will look smooth and attractive. If your local home center doesn't stock Baltic birch, find it at any hardwood specialty store.

If you choose, you can make the sides of the rollout drawers from any 1x4 solid wood that matches your cabinets and then finish to match (use plywood for the bases). But if you use 3/4-in. material for the sides, subtract 3 in. from the opening to size the rollout (not 2-1/2 in., as described in Photo 2 and Figure A).

The drawer carriers (Figure A) are made from pine 1x4s for the sides (Photo 7) and 1/4-in. MDF (medium-density fiberboard) for the bottoms (Photo 9). The MDF keeps the drawer bottom spaced properly while you shim and attach it to the cabinet sides. It can be removed and reused for other carriers after installation. If MDF isn't available, substitute any other 1/4-in. hardboard or plywood.

Side-mounted slides are the best choice among drawer slide options. Their ball-bearing mechanisms and precise fit make for smooth-operating drawers that hold 90 lbs. or more. Shown here are 22-in. full-extension side-mount drawer slides that have a 90-lb. weight rating. That means they'll be sturdy enough even for a drawer full of canned goods. Full-extension slides allow the rollout to extend completely past the cabinet front so you can access all the contents. You can find slides at any home center or well-stocked hardware store.

Measure carefully before you build

Nearly all standard base cabinets are 23-1/4 in. deep from the inside of the face frame (Photo 1) to the back of the cabinet. So in most cases, 22-in.-long rollout drawer and carrier sides will clear with room to spare. Check your cabinets to make sure that 22-in. rollouts will work. If you have shallower cabinets, subtract whatever is necessary when you build your rollouts and their carriers (see Figure A).

Then measure the cabinet width. The drawer has to clear the narrowest part of the

1 Open the cabinet doors to their widest point and measure the narrowest part of the cabinet opening (usually at the hinges).

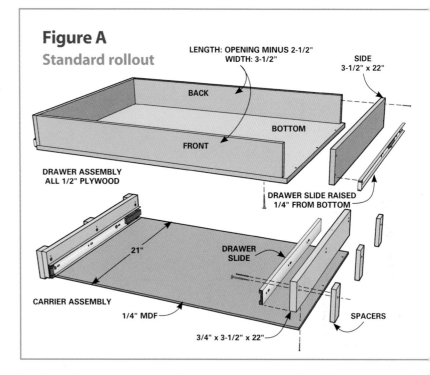

Figure A
Standard rollout

LENGTH: OPENING MINUS 2-1/2"
WIDTH: 3-1/2"

SIDE 3-1/2" x 22"

BACK

BOTTOM

FRONT

DRAWER ASSEMBLY ALL 1/2" PLYWOOD

DRAWER SLIDE RAISED 1/4" FROM BOTTOM

21"

DRAWER SLIDE

CARRIER ASSEMBLY

1/4" MDF

SPACERS

3/4" x 3-1/2" x 22"

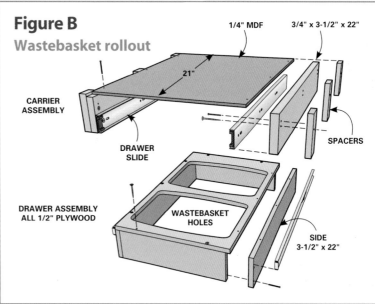

Figure B
Wastebasket rollout

1/4" MDF

3/4" x 3-1/2" x 22"

21"

CARRIER ASSEMBLY

DRAWER SLIDE

SPACERS

DRAWER ASSEMBLY ALL 1/2" PLYWOOD

WASTEBASKET HOLES

SIDE 3-1/2" x 22"

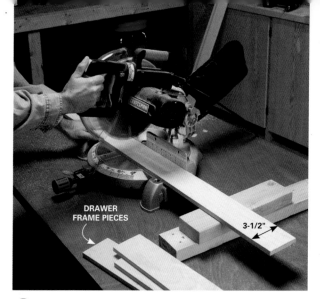

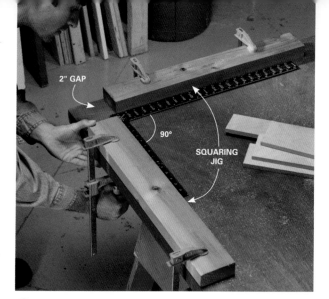

2 Rip 1/2-in. plywood down to 3-1/2 in. wide and cut two 22-in. lengths (drawer sides) and two more to the measured width minus 2-1/2 in. (drawer front and back; Figure A).

3 Clamp or screw two straight 24-in. 2x4s to the corner of a flat surface to use as a squaring jig. Use a carpenter's square to ensure squareness. Leave a 2-in. gap at the corner.

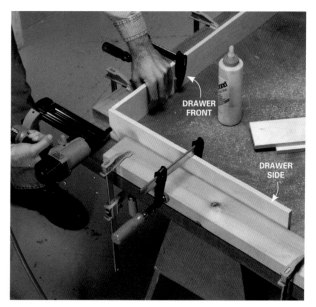

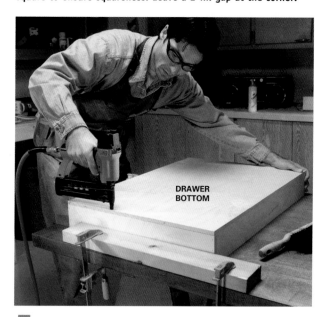

4 Spread wood glue on the ends and clamp a drawer side and front in place, then pin the corner together with three 1-1/4-in. brads. Repeat for the other three corners.

5 Cut a 1/2-in. plywood bottom to size. Apply a thin bead of glue to the bottom edges and nail one edge of the plywood flush with a side, spacing nails every 4 in. Then push the frame against the jig to square it and nail the other three edges.

opening (Photo 1). When taking this measurement, include hinges that protrude into the opening, the edge of the door attached to the hinges and even the doors that won't open completely because they hit nearby appliances or other cabinets. Plan on making the drawer front and rear parts 2-1/2 in. shorter than the opening (Figure A).

Shown here are drawers with 3-1/2-in.-high sides, but you can customize your own. Plan on higher sides for lightweight plastic storage containers or other tall or tippy items, and lower sides for stable, heavier items like small appliances.

Drawer slides aren't as confusing as they may seem

At first glance, drawer slides are pretty hard to figure out, but after you install one set, you'll be an expert. They're sold in

pairs and each of the pairs has two parts. The "drawer part" attaches to the rollout while the "cabinet part" attaches to the carrier. To separate them for mounting, slide them out to full length and then push, pull or depress a plastic release to separate the two parts. The cabinet part, which always encloses the drawer part, is the larger of the two, and the mounting screw hole locations will be shown in the directions. (Screws are included with the drawer slides.) The oversized holes allow for some adjustment, but if you follow the instructions, you shouldn't have to fuss with fine-tuning later. When mounting the slides, you should make sure to hold them flush with the front of the rollout drawer and carrier sides (Photos 6 and 7). The front of the drawer part usually has a bent metal stop that faces the front of the drawer.

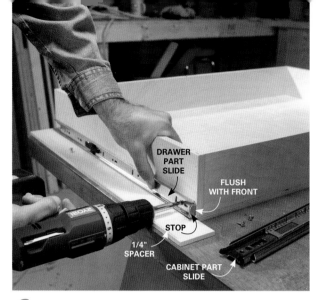

6 Separate the drawer slides and space the drawer part 1/4 in. up from the bottom. Hold it flush to the front and screw it to the rollout side.

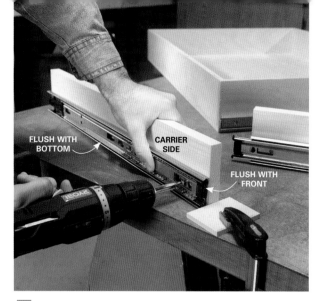

7 Mount the carrier part of the drawer slide flush with the bottom and front of the carrier sides.

8 Slide the drawer and carrier sides together and measure the carrier width. Cut 1/4-in. MDF to that width and 1 in. less than the carrier depth (usually 21 in.).

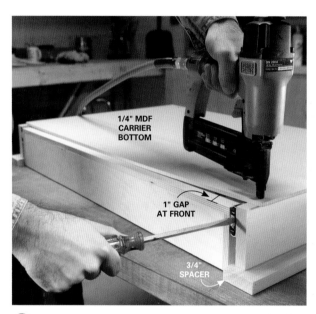

9 Rest the carrier assembly on 3/4-in.-thick spacers, pull the carrier sides slightly away from the drawer, then nail on the carrier bottom (no glue).

Assembling parts and finishing the rollouts

It's important to build the rollout drawers perfectly square for them to operate properly. Photos 3 and 4 show a simple squaring jig that you can clamp to a corner of any workbench to help. Use the jig to nail the frame together, but even more important, to hold the frame square when you nail on the bottom panel. If it hangs over the sides even a little, the drawer slides won't work smoothly.

Use 1-1/4-in. brads for all of the assembly. Glue the drawer parts together but not the bottom of the carrier. It only serves as a temporary spacer for mounting. (After mounting the carrier and drawer, you can remove it if it catches items on underlying drawers or even reuse it for other carriers.) If you'd like to finish the rollout for a richer look and easier cleaning, sand the edges with 120-grit paper and apply a couple of coats of water-based polyurethane before mounting the slides.

To figure the spacer thickness, rest the lower carrier on the bottom of the shelf, push it against one side of the cabinet and measure the gap on the other (Photo 10). Rip spacers to half that measurement and cut six of them to 3-1/2 in. long. Slip the spacers between both sides of the carrier to check the fit. They should slide in snugly but not tightly. Recut new spacers if needed. In out-of-square cabinets, you may have to custom-cut spacers for each of the three pairs of spacers, so check each of the three spacer positions. It's easiest to tack the spacers to the rollouts to hold them in place before predrilling 1/8-in. holes and running the screws through the rollout frames and spacers and into the cabinet sides (Photo 11).

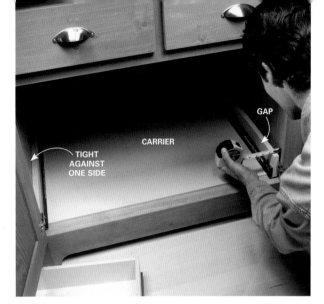

GAP

CARRIER

TIGHT AGAINST ONE SIDE

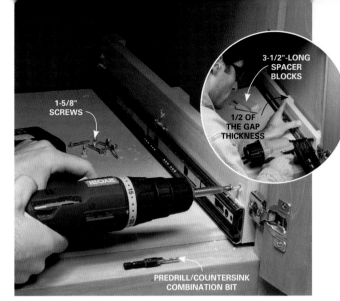

3-1/2"-LONG SPACER BLOCKS

1/2 OF THE GAP THICKNESS

1-5/8" SCREWS

PREDRILL/COUNTERSINK COMBINATION BIT

10 Remove the drawer, tip the carrier into the cabinet and push the carrier against one side. Measure the gap and rip six 3-1/2-in.-long spacers to half of the thickness.

11 Nail the spacers to the center and each end of the carrier sides (not into the cabinet; see inset photo). Then predrill and screw the carrier sides to the cabinet in the center of each shim. Slide the drawer back into place.

7" SPACER

7" SPACER

1/2" INSIDE TRACING

12 Cut plywood spacers to temporarily support the upper rollout and set them onto the carrier below. Rest the second carrier on the spacers and install it as shown in Photo 11.

13 Build an upside-down version of the carrier and rollouts for the wastebasket drawer (Figure B). Center and trace around the rim of the wastebasket(s). Use a compass to mark the opening 1/2 in. smaller.

Slip the rollout into its carrier and check for smooth operation. If you followed the process, it should work perfectly. If it binds, it's probably because the spacers are too wide or narrow. Pull out the carrier, remove the spacers and start the spacer process all over again.

The best way to level and fasten the upper rollout is to support it on temporary plywood spacers (Photo 12). The photo shows pieces of plywood cut 7 in. high. In reality, the exact height is up to you. If, for example, you want to store tall boxes of cereal on the bottom rollout and shorter items on the top, space the top rollout higher. You can even build and install three or more rollouts in one cabinet for mega-storage of short items like cans, cutlery or beverages. (Those now-obsolete shelves you're replacing with rollouts are good stock

to use for your spacers.) Again, pin the spacers in place with a brad or two to hold them while you're predrilling and screwing the carriers to the cabinet sides. Be sure to select screw lengths that won't penetrate exposed cabinet sides! In most cases, 1-5/8-in. screws are the best choice. Strive for 1/2-in. penetration into the cabinet sides. Countersink the heads as far as necessary to get the proper penetration.

Building wastebasket rollouts

Wastebasket rollouts are just upside-down versions of standard rollouts. That is, the carrier is mounted on the top rather than the bottom of the rollout and the slides are positioned at the bottom edge of the carrier sides. That lets the wastebasket lip clear the MDF. Follow Figure B on p. 7 for the details.

14 Drill 1/2-in. starting holes and cut the openings with a jigsaw.

CENTER DIVIDER

ADDED PANEL

Building rollouts in cabinets with center dividers

Many two-door cabinets have a center divider (photo above), which calls for a slightly different strategy. You can still build rollouts, but they'll be narrower versions on each side of the divider. (Check to be sure they won't be so narrow that they're impractical.) The key is to install a 3/4-in. plywood, particleboard or MDF panel between the center divider and the cabinet back to support the carriers.

Cut the panel to fit loosely between the divider and the cabinet back and high enough to support the top rollout position. Center the panel on the back side and middle of the divider and screw it into place with 1-in. angle brackets (they're completely out of sight). Use a carpenter's square to position the panel perfectly centered and vertical on the cabinet back and anchor it there, again using angle brackets. Measure, build and install the rollouts as shown here.

15 Mount the wastebasket carrier and drawer as shown in Photos 10 and 11.

This wastebasket rollout is built inside an 18-in.-wide cabinet, so it fits two plastic containers back to back. If you only have a 15-in. cabinet to work with, you may be limited to one container mounted sideways. Buy your containers ahead of time to fit your opening.

With some wastebasket rollouts, you may need to knock the MDF free from the carriers after mounting so the wastebasket lips will clear. That's OK; it won't affect operation.

It may not always work to center rollout assemblies in all openings with equal spacers on each side. That's especially true with narrow single cabinets that only have one pair of hinges. It's best to test things before permanent mounting. But if you make a mistake, it's a simple matter to unscrew the assembly, adjust the shims and remount everything.

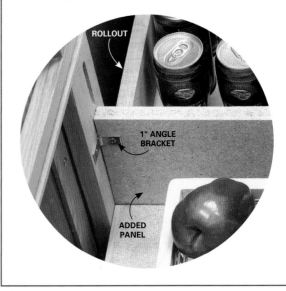

ROLLOUT

1" ANGLE BRACKET

ADDED PANEL

Built-in bath cabinet

If you're short on bathroom storage space, this built-in cabinet could be just the ticket. It's large and spacious, yet the shallow depth allows easy viewing and access to all of the contents. No more digging around in drawers or the dark corners of linen closets to find what you need. And since it's recessed into the wall, you won't lose any valuable floor space.

This project is a great introduction to basic cabinet-building skills. It's a simple box with a face frame attached to the front. You buy the doors in the style that best fits your bathroom décor and mount them to the face frame. The doors shown here came complete with 35mm holes to accept the concealed Euro-style hinges. These hinges are great for novice cabinetmakers because they allow you to adjust the doors for a perfect fit.

Here you'll learn the entire cabinet assembly process. Then you'll see how to cut a hole in your wall and safely remove a stud to create a recessed space for the cabinet. Even with little woodworking experience, you should be able to complete the cabinet in a day. Applying the finish and installing the cabinet will take another five or six hours.

You could cut the cabinet sides and face frame parts with a circular saw and saw guide, but you'll get tighter-fitting joints if you use a power miter saw or a table saw with a miter gauge. For the cabinet shown, a pocket hole jig and pocket screws were used to assemble the face frame pieces and attach it to the box. If you don't own a pocket hole jig, glue and nail the face frame to the cabinet box with finish nails.

Including the doors, door glass and glass shelves, this cabinet cost about $400 to $500. If you use oak instead of cherry, you could build it for less. Patterned glass and glass shelves for the doors can be ordered from a local glass company or an online retailer. Euro-style mounting plates are available at woodworking stores and online.

WHAT IT TAKES

Time: 1 weekend
Skill level: Intermediate

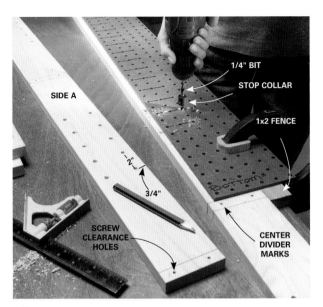

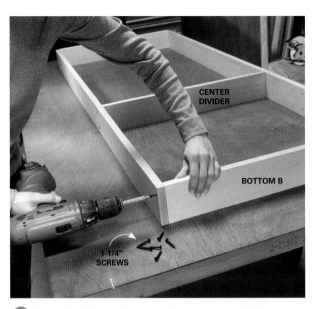

1 Cut the cabinet box pieces (A and B; Figure A on p. 14) to length. Mark the location of the center divider on the side pieces and drill screw-clearance holes. Also drill holes for the adjustable shelf supports using a pegboard jig.

2 Screw the sides to the top and bottom through the pre-drilled clearance holes. Then line up the middle horizontal divider with the marks and screw it in.

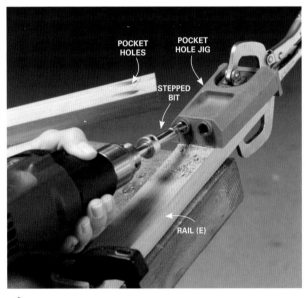

3 Align one edge of the 1/4-in. plywood back with the side of the cabinet. Predrill the screw holes and screw it into place with 1-in. screws. Then square the cabinet and screw the other three edges and center divider.

4 Cut the face frame parts to length (D and E). Drill pocket screw holes on the back side of the rails (E) with a special stepped bit and pocket hole jig.

Choose the cabinet location carefully

Before you order doors or start building the cabinet, make sure you have a good spot to install the cabinet. Exterior walls are out. There's likely to be insulation in them, and there may be structural issues to deal with as well. Look for a space that's about 26 in. wide and 68 in. high. After you've found a potential location, use a stud finder to locate the studs, then mark them with masking tape. Position the cabinet so that you only have to remove one stud. You can put your cabinet at any height. The top of this cabinet lines up with the door, 80 in. above the floor.

Then make sure the spot you chose doesn't have any hid-

den obstructions. The easiest method is to cut two 6-in. square inspection holes in the drywall, one on each side of the stud you'll be removing. Then look in with a flashlight to make sure there aren't any electrical wires, plumbing pipes or heat ducts in the way. A less invasive but also less thorough method is to poke a bent clothes hanger through a hole in the wall and probe around. You'll have to do this in several places, though. If space is tight, you may have to adjust the cabinet dimensions to fit it in. When you've found a location, order the doors and hinges. If the door sizes are different from those shown here, adjust the cabinet sizes to fit them. The doors overlap the face frame 3/4 in. on all sides.

Figure A Built-in bath cabinet details

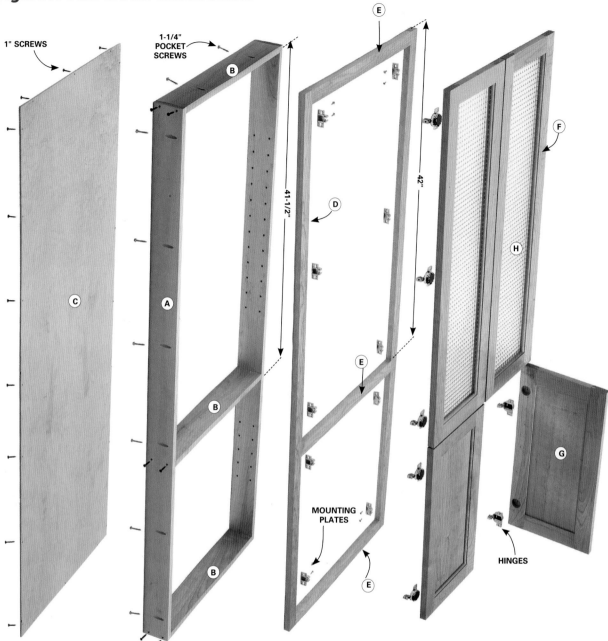

1" SCREWS

1-1/4" POCKET SCREWS

41-1/2"

42"

MOUNTING PLATES

HINGES

A B C D E F G H

Shopping list for wall opening

ITEM	QTY.
2x4 x 8' studs	3
Metal angle brackets	2
Small container of No. 8 x 1-1/4" pocket screws	1
2-1/2" drywall or cabinet screws	12
Joint compound for patching	
1/2" plywood scrap	
1-1/4" drywall screws	

Cutting list

KEY	PCS.	SIZE & DESCRIPTION
A	2	3/4" x 3-1/2" x 66-3/8" maple (sides)
B	3	3/4" x 3-1/2" x 22-7/8" maple (top, bottom, middle)
C	1	1/4" x 24-3/8" x 66-3/8" birch plywood (back)
D	2	3/4" x 1-1/2" x 67-5/8" cherry (face frame stiles)
E	3	3/4" x 1-1/2" x 22-5/8" cherry (face frame rails)
F	2	3/4" x 12" x 42" cherry doors
G	2	3/4" x 12" x 24" cherry doors
H	2	patterned glass inserts to fit doors
J	5	polished-edge glass shelves

5 Align the face frame parts (D and E). Clamp them and join them with pocket screws.

6 Drill pocket screw holes on the outside of the cabinet box (parts A and B). Center the frame on the cabinet box (it should overlap the inside 1/8 in.), clamp it and attach it with pocket screws.

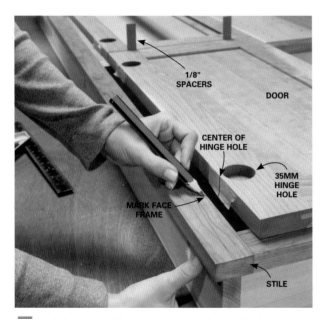

7 Mark the hinge hole centers on the edge of the doors with a combination square. Set two doors in place and transfer the hinge center locations to the face frame stile. For the other set of doors, transfer these marks to the opposite stile by measuring from the bottom of the face frame.

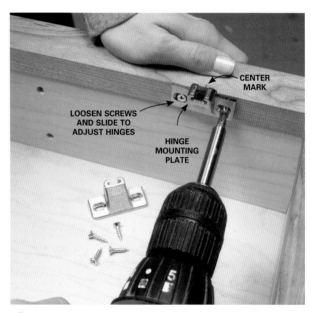

8 Center the hinge mounting plates on these marks, predrill and screw them to the face frame. Center the screws in the slots to allow adjustments up and down.

Build the box first

Start by cutting the 1x4 cabinet sides (A), and top, center and bottom (B) to length. Then use a square to mark the location of the center divider on the sides (Photo 1). Drill 5/32-in. screw-clearance holes through the sides at these marks and at the top and bottom. Complete the side pieces by drilling the shelf pin holes. Make a drilling jig by screwing a 1x2 fence to a strip of pegboard (make sure the pegboard has 1/4-in. holes). Position the edge of the 1x2 fence 3/4 in. from the center of the first row of holes. Use a 1/4-in. brad point bit to drill the holes.

Tighten a drill stop collar onto the bit to limit the depth of the holes to the thickness of the pegboard plus 1/2 in. Skip every other set of holes to create holes that are 2 in. apart. Be careful to mark the bottom of the jig and align it the same for both sides to ensure that the holes line up.

Screw the sides to the top, bottom and middle piece with 1-1/4-in. screws (Photo 2). Then cut 1/4-in. plywood for the back and attach it with 1-in. screws (Photo 3). Make sure the plywood back is perfectly square. Then align the cabinet edges with it to square the cabinet.

COMPACT EURO HINGE

9 Line up the hinge parallel to the door's edge and screw the hinges to the doors.

INSPECTION HOLE

PLUMB LINE

DRYWALL KEYHOLE SAW

10 Mark the cutout dimensions on the wall. Cut along the lines with a drywall keyhole saw.

Assemble the face frame and attach it to the cabinet box

Start with 1x2s that are milled accurately with square edges. Home centers and lumberyards usually stock a few species of hardwood 1x2s, but cherry may be a little harder to find. Check hardwood lumber suppliers online or call a local cabinetmaker to find a source. Sight down the boards to make sure they're perfectly straight. Then use a miter saw or table saw to cut the pieces to length, making sure the end cuts are perfectly square. Arrange the face frame parts with the best-looking face down and make a pencil mark on the back of each piece. Using a pocket hole jig with a stepped drill bit, drill a pair of holes in both ends of the rails (Photo 4). Drill on the back, or marked, side. Complete the face frame by clamping the joints one at a time and joining them with 1-1/4-in. pocket screws (Photo 5). If you haven't used a pocket hole jig before, practice on scrap wood. You'll quickly get the hang of it.

Drill pocket holes around the outside of the cabinet box and attach the face frame with pocket screws (Photo 6). The face frame is sized to overlap the interior of the cabinet box by 1/8 in. Make sure this overlap is even all the way around, then clamp it before you attach the face frame. If you don't own a pocket hole jig, you can nail the face frame to the box with 6d finish nails and fill the holes later with putty in a matching color.

Attach the hinge mounting plates accurately

The hinges fit into the round holes bored in the doors and mount to a separate mounting plate that you'll screw to the face frame. Positioning them is a bit tricky. The first step is to attach the mounting plates to the edge of the face frame. Start by marking the center of each hole on a piece of masking tape stuck to the door's edge (Photo 7). Use a square to mark the center of the hinge hole on the edge of the door. Then set one upper and one lower door in place, making sure they overlap the face frame on the top and bottom by 3/4 in. Leave a 1/8-in.

gap between them (use a 1/8-in. spacer). Then mark the hinge centers on the face frame (Photo 7). After marking one side, use exact measurements to duplicate the hinge center positions on the other side. Finally, center the mounting plates on these marks and screw them to the edge of the face frame (Photo 8).

Mount the hinges next. Press the hinges into the holes and use a square to make sure the screw holes are parallel to the edge of the door (Photo 9). Then drive the mounting screws.

Cut the hole for the cabinet

In most cases, you'll have to remove a stud to make a wide enough opening (Photos 10–12). Photos 13 and 14 show how to add a header to support the cutoff stud. The metal angle brackets support the new header. The sill and side pieces aren't structural but provide backing for the drywall and a place to attach the cabinet.

Use a level and pencil to mark the cutout dimensions on the wall (Photo 10). Mark the outline 1/4 in. taller and wider than the cabinet box dimensions. Cut the drywall along the lines with a drywall saw and break it out.

The next step is to cut out the stud to make room for the header (Photos 11 and 12). Make a short level line 3-3/4 in. above the top of the cutout opening and centered over the stud. This is where you'll cut the stud to allow room for the header to fit under it. Make a similar line 1-1/2 in. below the bottom of the cutout. Cut through the stud at each spot (Photo 11). If you're careful to control the depth of the blade, you may be able to cut through the stud without cutting through the drywall on the opposite side. But don't worry. If you do cut through, the thin slot will be easy to patch.

Remove the cutout section of stud by hitting it hard with a hammer on the edge nearest you to twist the nails or screws loose from the drywall on the opposite side (Photo 12). Measure the distance between the remaining wall studs and cut two 2x4s 3/16 in. shorter than the measurement. Build

11 Draw horizontal lines 3-3/4 in. above and 1-1/2 in. below the opening at the stud location. Cut through the stud at these lines with a reciprocating saw or handsaw. Also cut the stud in the middle to simplify removal.

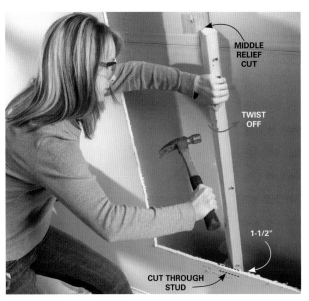

12 Pound on the corner of the cutoff stud to twist it away from the drywall. Pull it out of the opening.

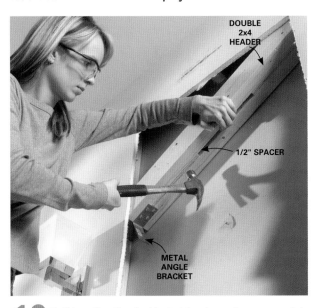

13 Nail together the double 2x4 header and screw a metal angle bracket to one end. Slide it into position against the cutoff stud and level the header.

14 Screw the metal angle bracket to the stud. Screw another special angle bracket to the opposite end of the header and to the stud.

Shopping list

ITEM	QTY.	ITEM	QTY.
1x4 x 6' birch or maple (A, B)	3	3-3/8" x 22-3/4" x 3/8" polished-edge glass shelves	5
1x2 x 6' cherry (D, E)	3	Shelf supports	20
4' x 8' x 1/4" birch plywood (C)	1	1-1/4" drywall or cabinet screws	12
12" x 42" cabinet doors (F)	2	1" drywall or cabinet screws	24
12" x 24" cabinet doors (G)	2	1-1/4" pocket screws	30
Pieces of patterned glass for doors	2	1-1/4" trim head screws (mount cabinet)	4
Compact Euro-style face frame hinges	10	Cabinet handles	4
3/4" overlay mounting plates	10	Polyurethane finish	1 qt.

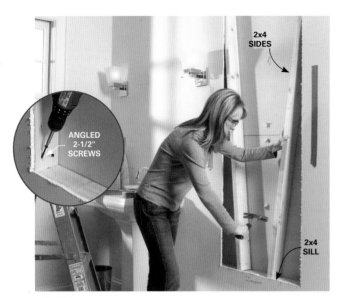

2x4
SIDES

ANGLED
2-1/2"
SCREWS

2x4
SILL

15 Nail a 2x4 sill to the cutoff stud. Level it and drive angled screws into the studs at each end. Cut 2x4s to fit between the header and the sill and fasten them even with the drywall edges with angled screws.

TRIM HEAD
SCREW

16 Slide the cabinet into the opening and level it. Secure it with trim screws driven through the sides into the framing. Conceal the screws by driving them into shelf pin holes.

the 2x4 header by sandwiching scraps of 1/2-in. plywood or 1/2-in. strips of wood between the 2x4s and nailing them together with 12d nails. Slide the header up against the cutoff stud (Photo 13) and hold it temporarily in place with a screw through the drywall. Level the header and support it by screwing metal angle brackets to the studs with 1-1/4-in. screws (Photos 13 and 14). Cut a 2x4 the same length as the header for the sill, level it and attach it to the studs with 2-1/2-in. screws driven at an angle. Complete the framing by cutting 2x4s to fit between the header and sill on each side of the cabinet and securing them with angled 2-1/2-in. screws (Photo 15). Predrill to keep the sides from slipping back too far (Photo 15 inset).

Finish up by mounting the cabinet

It's easiest to sand and finish the cabinet before mounting it to the wall. Apply stain if you desire and three coats of polyurethane varnish. Then just slip the cabinet into the opening, level it and screw it into the framing on each side (Photo 16). Don't overtighten or you'll pull the frame out of square. Remount the doors and adjust the hinges so the space between the doors is even (Photo 17). The top doors shown here were ordered to accommodate 1/8-in. glass. They came with a clear plastic strip that slid into a slot to hold the glass in place. Make sure to get recommendations from your door supplier for securing the glass in the door you order.

17 Reinstall the doors and adjust them until the space between the doors is even. Loosen the base plate screws to move a door up and down. Loosen the hinge screw to adjust the doors sideways.

Great Goofs

Cutting corners

Not long ago, we remodeled our kitchen, complete with new cabinets. I prepped the room, and when the new cabinets were delivered, I jumped right in and started hanging the upper cabinets first. They went in nicely, so I began carrying in the base cabinets. No matter which way I turned the corner base cabinet, complete with the lazy Susan, I couldn't get it into the kitchen. The entry doors to the kitchen were 32 in. wide, and there was no way that cabinet was going to fit. Finally I hauled out my reciprocating saw and cut into the back of my $450 cabinet. Fortunately, my carpentry reputation is still intact, because once the countertops and doors were on and the lazy Susan was filled, nobody could see the patchwork behind.

Mirror, mirror on the wall

Last holiday season, I bought my husband a fog-proof mirror for shaving. Noticing that he wasn't as closely shaved as he used to be, I asked him how he liked it. He said, "Just fine." Not really believing him, I went to investigate. I noticed what looked like a crack near the edge of the glass. After running my fingernail across it, I realized it was a protective film. I peeled it off. The next day my husband commented that he liked the new mirror better than the old one! He looked better-groomed as well.

Unplanned improvement

When updating our old kitchen cabinets with new hardware, I had to shift one of the old hole locations for the cabinet pull screws. I used the countertop as a makeshift workbench and began drilling holes in the doors and drawer fronts. I was being careful to let the doors overhang the countertop as I drilled. When I reached the last set of doors, the drilling felt tougher. This door somehow seemed thicker. As I pulled out the drill, I discovered that the bit had gone right through the countertop! Not being able to disguise this nasty blemish, I cut out a section of the countertop and made a cutting board insert. Everyone tells me how clever the new cutting board inlay is, but I just nod my head and keep the rest of the story to myself!

He blew it, all right

Not long ago, our refrigerator was cooling poorly, so I loosened the grille cover on the bottom of the fridge. Sure enough, I'd neglected that cleaning job way too long. The cooling coils were packed with dust. After failed attempts to rig up small tubing to the shop vacuum to clean between the coils, I went to the garage to find a better solution. The leaf blower caught my eye, so I brought it inside, plugged it in and aimed it at the coils and turned it on. Before I could switch to the low speed, a huge cloud of dust had billowed out from behind the fridge and covered the whole kitchen. Luckily, my wife wasn't home at the time. I got out the vacuum and spent more than an hour frantically cleaning. Later that day, she opened the cupboard above the fridge and asked me why there was a layer of dust and soot covering everything inside. I now use the leaf blower for outside work only.

Above-cabinet shelving

Make every inch count with an easy-to-clean upper-cabinet shelf

If you have empty space above your kitchen cabinets, you already know how difficult it is to keep it clean. And if you've ever tried to display anything above them, you also know the surface isn't flat, so objects sink out of view. Why not solve both problems with an attractive display shelf you can easily build in a day?

This project only requires basic carpentry tools and skills. Even the miter joints can be cut with a simple handsaw miter box. We used an 18-gauge finish nailer to make the job go faster, but you can just as easily predrill and hand-nail. And don't worry about trying to match your cabinet's finish or wood type. The shelf will look great if you paint it to match another accent color in the room.

Cutting list

KEY	SIZE & DESCRIPTION
A	3/4" x 1-1/4" board cut 1-1/2" shorter than the cabinet face width
B	3/4" x 1-1/4" board cut the same as cabinet depth
C	3/4" plywood cut 3" longer than the cabinet face width and 1-1/2" deeper than the cabinet depth
D	1/4" x 3/4" molding cut and mitered to cover exposed plywood
E	Filler piece to fill void between the face frame and the wall
F	2-1/4" crown molding cut and mitered to fit over cabinet face and under shelf

Figure A
Shelf details

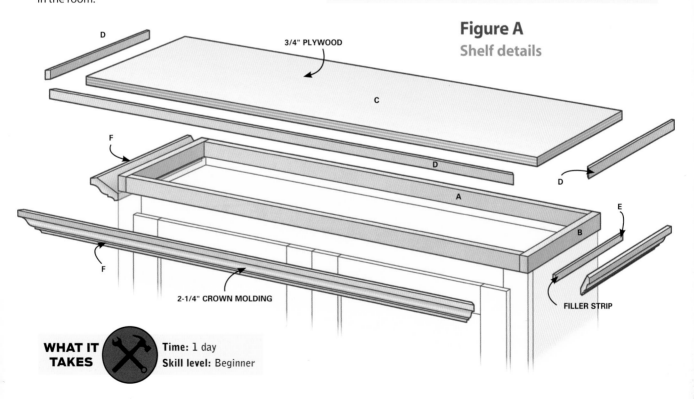

D

3/4" PLYWOOD

C

D

A

D

F

E

B

F

2-1/4" CROWN MOLDING

FILLER STRIP

WHAT IT TAKES
Time: 1 day
Skill level: Beginner

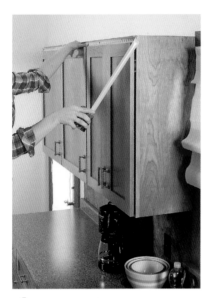

1 Measure the tops of your cabinets to determine your materials list. Also check the distance above the cabinet doors to determine the support cleat height for the shelf.

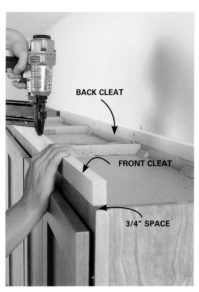

2 Nail cleats to the tops of the cabinets to elevate the shelf. Leave 3/4 in. of space on each side for the side cleats. The side cleats will overhang on the cabinet side.

BACK CLEAT
FRONT CLEAT
3/4" SPACE

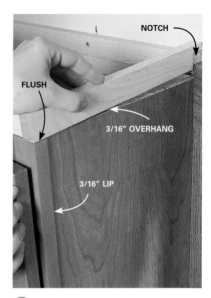

3 Fit the side cleats so there's a consistent overhang on the edge. We had to notch the cleat to fit behind the window molding.

NOTCH
FLUSH
3/16" OVERHANG
3/16" LIP

Get what you need at the lumberyard

The best material for the main shelf is 3/4-in. plywood (Photo 4). Get a finished grade that is smooth and easy to sand. The cleats under the shelf (Photo 2) are fillers to elevate the shelf just enough so the crown molding fits under the shelf and yet comfortably clears the doors below. We had about 1 in. of space above the doors, so we needed cleats that were 1-1/4 in. high. If you don't have access to a table saw, you can carefully cut them with your circular saw and an edge guide. Besides the 2-1/4-in. crown molding, you'll need trim to cover the edge of the plywood (Photo 6) for a finished look. You can use "screen"

molding or "parting stop," or just rip a strip from a wider board to 1/4 in. or thicker. Just follow the photos for details about sizing and fitting the pieces.

Paint your molding to match

Finish up by filling your nail holes and sanding the wood with 150-grit sandpaper. Prime the wood and then select a satin or gloss paint finish that'll be easy to wipe clean. Because it's difficult to get an exact cabinet color match for natural wood cabinets, simply pick a color that will accent your kitchen countertops or cabinets.

3/4" PLYWOOD TOP
CONSISTENT OVERHANG

4 Measure and cut the top from 3/4-in. plywood, overhanging 1-1/2 in. on the front and each side.

1-1/2" OVERHANG

5 Nail the top to the cleats with 2-in. finish nails. Make sure the overhang is even on each side.

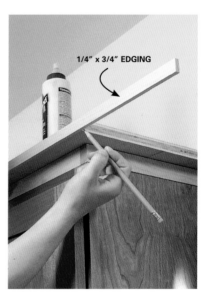

1/4" x 3/4" EDGING

6 Glue and nail the 3/4-in.-wide edge molding to the exposed plywood edges. Miter the corners for a more finished appearance.

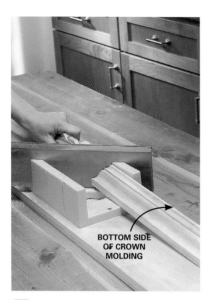

BOTTOM SIDE OF CROWN MOLDING

GLUED AND NAILED EDGING

2-1/4" CROWN MOLDING

NAIL HERE FIRST

FILLER STRIP

7 Position your molding upside down in the miter box to support both the top and the bottom of the molding. Check the direction of the angle twice before you cut.

8 Nail the crown molding to the face of the cabinet and up into the shelf at an angle. The molding will completely cover the cuts.

9 Fit the side pieces of crown molding and slip a 3/16-in.-thick filler strip under the front edge to hide the gap created by the face frame overhang.

Organize your knives

Store your kitchen cutlery in style with this handsome knife block. It's fast, easy and fun to build, and includes a 6-in.-wide storage box for a knife sharpener.

To build one, you only need a 3/4-in. x 8-in. x 4-ft. hardwood board and a 6-in. x 6-1/2-in. piece of 1/4-in. hardwood plywood to match.

Begin by cutting off a 10-in. length of the board and setting it aside. Rip the remaining 38-in. board to 6 in. wide and cut five evenly spaced saw kerfs 5/8 in. deep along one face. Crosscut the slotted board into four 9-in. pieces and glue them into a block, being careful not to slop glue into the saw kerfs (you can clean them out with a knife before the glue dries). Saw a 15-degree angle on one end and screw the plywood piece under the angled end of the block.

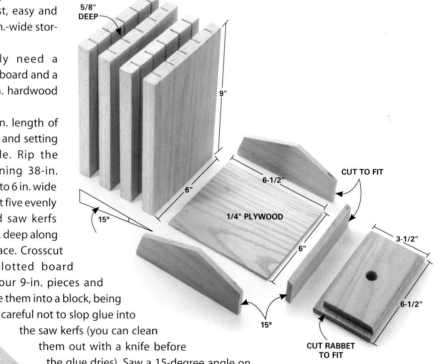

5/8" DEEP

9"

6"

15°

6-1/2"

CUT TO FIT

1/4" PLYWOOD

6"

3-1/2"

6-1/2"

15°

CUT RABBET TO FIT

Cut the 6-1/2-in. x 3-in. lid from the leftover board and slice the remaining piece into 1/4-in.-thick pieces for the sides and end of the box. Glue them around the plywood floor. Cut a rabbet on three sides of the lid so it fits snugly on the box and drill a 5/8-in. hole for a finger pull. Then just add a finish and you're set for years of happy carving!

Kitchen organization tips

Find extra space

A corner appliance cabinet hides coffeemakers, toasters and other small appliances while making efficient use of often-wasted corner space.

The above-refrigerator cabinet contains vertical partitions for storing trays, flat pans and cutting boards.

Double-decker drawers with sliding trays store two layers of knives, utilizing valuable drawer "dead air" space.

Swinging trash

Here's a space-saving solution to the kitchen or bathroom wastebasket problem. Screw wire shelf anchor clips to the inside of the door and hook the lip of a small wastebasket right on the hooks.

WIRE SHELF ANCHOR CLIPS

Keep your spray bottles in line

It can be hard to keep spray bottles from falling over and making a mess under your bathroom or kitchen sink. To keep them upright, hang them from a short tension rod (sold at discount stores) in your cabinet.

Home office & technolgy

Ultimate office organizer

Convert a spare closet into super-organized office storage

Is your home office a mess? Do you need a spot to organize your kids' schoolwork and projects? Or do you just want to get your office stuff out of sight when you have guests? We'll show you how to solve all these problems by converting a spare closet into a super-organized space.

In this story, we'll show you how to build and install wall shelf cabinets, a countertop and under-mount drawers, including how to adjust the dimensions to fit these projects in your closet. We'll also show you an easy way to conceal all those cords that usually dangle down behind the desk. We've included a Materials List on p. 29, but you'll have to adjust the quantities to fit your closet. The project shown here is constructed with birch plywood and boards and cost us about $400.

This is a great project for any intermediate to advanced DIYer. There's no complicated joinery—the wall shelves and drawers are just wooden boxes that are screwed together. We used a table saw to cut the plywood, a narrow-crown staple gun to attach the shelf backs and drawer bottoms, and an 18-gauge nailer to attach the face frames. If you don't have these tools, you can use a circular saw and straightedge guide to cut the plywood, and a good old-fashioned hammer and nails. It will just take a little longer.

Simple construction, fantastic features

1 Brighten up your work surface with under-cabinet lights.

2 Hide the cords with a power strip tucked behind a backsplash.

3 Easy-to-build shelf units create tons of storage space.

4 The world's simplest drawers hang under the countertop.

1
UNDER-CABINET LIGHTS

3
SHELF UNITS

2
HIDDEN POWER SUPPLY

4
STORAGE DRAWERS

WHAT IT TAKES
Time: 1 weekend
Skill level: Intermediate

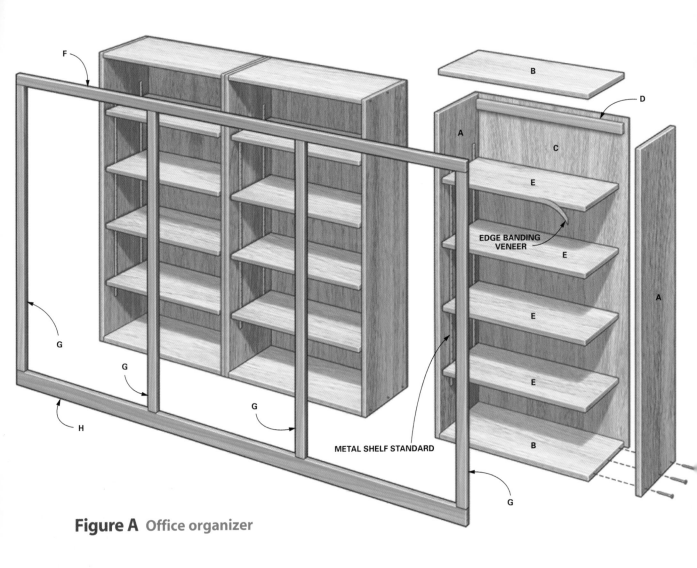

Figure A Office organizer

Cutting list

KEY	PCS.	SIZE & DESCRIPTION
Shelf cabinet		
A	6	11-1/4" x 47-3/4" x 3/4" plywood sides
B	6	11-1/4" x 26" x 3/4" plywood top, bottom*
C	3	27-1/2" x 47-3/4" x 1/4" plywood back
D	3	1-1/2" x 3/4" x 26" hanging strip
E	12	11-1/4" x 25-5/8" x 3/4" plywood shelves*
F	1	1-1/2" x 84" x 3/4" face frame
G	4	1-1/2" x 48" x 3/4" face frame **
H	1	2-1/2" x 84" x 3/4" face frame
Drawer frame		
J	4	3" x 57" x 3/4" plywood stringers
K	4	3" x 20" x 3/4" plywood dividers
Drawers		
L	4	7-1/4" x 20" x 3/4" plywood sides
M	4	7-1/4" x 15-1/2" x 3/4" plywood back and front*
N	2	17" x 20" x 1/4" plywood bottoms*

KEY	PCS.	SIZE & DESCRIPTION
Drawers (cont.)		
P	2	18-7/8" x 9" x 3/4" plywood fronts*
Q	2	2-1/4" x 20" x 3/4" plywood sides
R	2	2-1/4" x 15-1/2" x 3/4" back and front*
S	1	17" x 20" x 1/4" plywood bottom*
T	1	18-7/8" x 3/4" x 4" plywood front*
Countertop		
U	1	1-1/2" x 3/4" x 84" back support
V	2	1-1/2" x 3/4" x 23-1/4" side supports
W	2	24" x 84" x 3/4" plywood countertop **
X	1	2-1/4" x opening width x 3/4" face
Y	1	1" x 3/4" x 84" cleat
Z	1	4-3/8" x 84" x 3/4" backsplash

* Based on full 3/4" plywood. Adjust if your plywood is slightly thinner.

** Cut to fit.

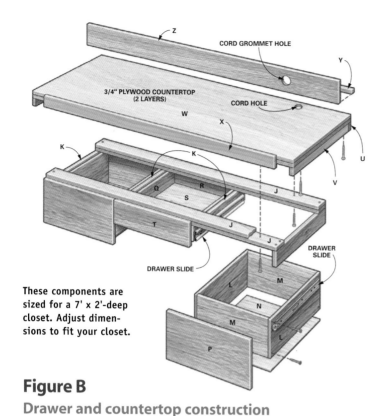

Labels in figure: Z, CORD GROMMET HOLE, Y, 3/4" PLYWOOD COUNTERTOP (2 LAYERS), CORD HOLE, W, X, K, K, U, V, Q, R, S, J, J, T, J, DRAWER SLIDE, DRAWER SLIDE, L, M, N, M, L, P

These components are sized for a 7' x 2'-deep closet. Adjust dimensions to fit your closet.

Figure B
Drawer and countertop construction

Materials list

ITEM	QTY.
4' x 8' x 3/4" plywood	4
4' x 8' x 1/4" plywood	2
1x2 x 8' boards	7
1x3 x 8' board	1
1x3 x 6' board (rip to 2-1/4")	1
1x6 x 8' board (rip to 4-3/8" for parts Y and Z)	1
Shelf standards	6
Shelf clips	48
20" full-extension drawer slide sets	3
Iron-on veneer edging	48 ft.
1-1/4" screws	
1-5/8" screws	
2-1/2" screws	
3" screws	
Finish nails or nail gun pins	
Wood glue	
Cord grommets	

CABINET SIDE

COUNTERTOP SUPPORT

1 Mark the walls and attach the countertop supports. Draw level lines for the bottom of the countertop and cabinets. Draw vertical lines to indicate the sides of the cabinets. Then screw countertop supports to studs at the back and sides of the closet.

Adjust the dimensions to fit your closet

Start by measuring the distance between the side walls. Keeping in mind that 32 in. is about the maximum width for a plywood shelf, decide how many shelf units you need. To figure out exactly how wide each cabinet should be, subtract 1-1/2 in. from the total measurement and divide the remainder by the number of cabinets. This will leave a 3/4-in. space between the cabinet and the wall at each end that you'll cover with the face frame. This 3/4-in. space makes it easy to install the shelf cabinets in the closet without worrying about an exact fit. We needed three 27-1/2-in.-wide cabinets to fit our 84-in.-wide closet. We built the cabinets 47-3/4 in. tall. If you have standard 8-ft.-tall walls, the cabinets will reach the ceiling. After you do the calculations, double-check your math by drawing lines on the closet wall. Draw a level line 28-1/2 in. from the floor to mark the bottom of the 1-1/2-in.-thick countertop. Then draw another line 47-1/2 in. from the floor for the bottom of the wall cabinets. Finally, draw vertical lines for the sides of the cabinets.

You'll also have to decide how wide to make the drawers. You can use the technique we show here to build drawers in a size and configuration that will work best in your closet. The key is to build the frame and mount the drawer slides before you build the drawers. Then you can measure between the slides (Photo 8) and build the drawers to fit.

Mount the countertop

The countertop is two layers of plywood that are glued and screwed together. It rests on cleats that are screwed to the wall studs. Start by measuring the closet interior at the level of the countertop. Use a framing square to check the corners. Deduct

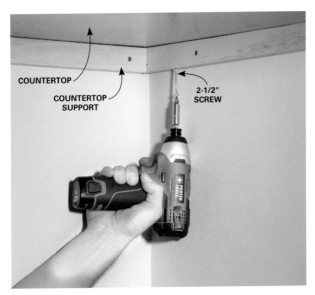

COUNTERTOP

COUNTERTOP SUPPORT

2-1/2" SCREW

2 Fasten the countertop. Screw through the countertop supports into the countertop. Lay something heavy on top, or ask a helper to press down while you drive the screws.

FACE BOARD

3 Cap the front edge. Glue and nail a board to the front edge to cover the plywood and add strength. Wipe off glue squeeze-out with a damp rag.

SHELF STANDARD

4 Assemble the wall cabinets. Mount shelf standards on the cabinet sides before assembly. Then screw the sides to the bottom and top with 1-5/8-in. screws. Drill pilot holes to prevent the plywood from splitting.

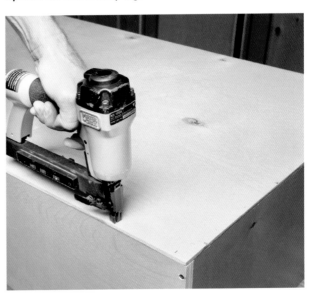

5 Square the cabinet with the plywood back. Use the plywood back as a guide for squaring the cabinet. Apply a bead of glue. Nail one edge of the plywood back to the cabinet side. Then adjust the cabinet box as needed to align the remaining edges and nail these.

1/4 in. from the length and depth to allow for the top to fit easily. You can cover any gaps with the backsplash. Transfer these measurements to your plywood and cut out the two pieces. Use less-expensive plywood for the bottom if you like. Screw 1x2 cleats to the back, side and front walls to support the top (Photo 1). Then drop the top into place and attach it from underneath with 2-1/2-in. screws (Photo 2). Finish the front edge with a 2-1/4-in.-wide board (Photo 3).

Build the wall shelf cabinets

Start by cutting the parts from the 4 x 8-ft. sheets of plywood. If you're using a table saw, keep the good side of the plywood facing up as you cut the parts. If you're using a circular saw,

face the good side down so that any splintering or chipping won't show. We think it's easier to finish the parts before you assemble them.

It's also easier to install the shelf standards to the cabinet sides before you put the cabinet together. Make sure the shelf standards are oriented the right way. We put a piece of masking tape on the top of each side to keep track. Here's a building tip you can use for the cabinet and drawer boxes: Nail the cabinet sides to the top and bottom before you drill pilot holes for the screws. The nails hold the parts in perfect alignment while you drill the holes and drive the 1-5/8-in. screws. Screw the sides to the top and bottom (Photo 4). Then nail on the back. If you were careful to cut the 1/4-in. plywood back accu-

1x2 LEDGER

6 Install the cabinets. Rest the bottom of the cabinet on the ledger and tilt the cabinet up. Drive 3-in. screws through the hanging strip at the top of the cabinet into the studs.

Wiring your closet—get help online!

We're not showing how to wire your closet office here, but chances are you'll want to add at least one electrical outlet and possibly cable, phone or network wiring. We've got tons of how-to information at our Web site to help you with these projects (you'll find one approach on p. 39). Go to familyhandyman.com and enter one of the search terms below.

To add an outlet, search for "electrical outlet." But keep in mind that the new National Electrical Code requires that closet outlets be arc fault protected. This means you'll have to either connect to or add a circuit that's protected by an arc fault circuit interrupter (AFCI). While you're adding wiring, don't forget about closet lighting (search for "lighting"). And for information on how to install coax, phone and Cat5e cable, search for "cable."

1x2

1x3

7 Finish the fronts. Nail a 1x3 to the lower cabinet edge to create a valance for under-cabinet lighting. Nail 1x2s to the cabinet top and sides to cover the raw plywood edges.

rately, you can square the cabinet by aligning it with the back before nailing it on (Photo 5). You'll cover the front edge of the cabinets with a wood face frame after they're mounted (Photo 7). Finish the front edge of the plywood shelves with iron-on edge banding. For complete instructions on installing edge banding, go to familyhandyman.com and search for "edge banding."

Start the cabinet installation by screwing a 1x2 ledger to the wall to support the wall cabinets. Align the top edge of the board with the 47-1/2-in.-high level line and drive a screw at each stud location. Next, measure from the vertical lines to the center of the wall studs, and transfer these measurements to the hanging strip at the top of each wall cabinet so you'll know where to drive the cabinet installation screws. Hang the cabinets by resting the bottom edge on the ledger, tipping them up against the wall, and driving 3-in. screws through the hanging strip into the studs (Photo 6). Secure the bottom of the cabinets by driving a nail or screw down into the ledger. Connect the fronts of the cabinets by hiding 1-1/4-in. screws under the shelf standards. Complete the installation by nailing on the face frames (Photo 7). We used a 1x3 for the bottom face frame to hide the under-cabinet lighting.

Build the drawers

You can buy drawer slides that mount directly to the underside of a desk or countertop, but we'll show you another method that allows you to use high-quality, side-mounted drawer slides. We bought these full-extension ball-bearing slides at the local home center. They cost about $15 per drawer. But you can substitute less-expensive epoxy-coated slides to save some money. You'll have to measure your closet to figure out the drawer sizes. Just make sure the drawers clear the open closet doors.

Building the drawer support frame is straightforward. Start by laying two of the stringers (J) side by side and marking the location of the drawer dividers (K) on them. Ball-bearing slides

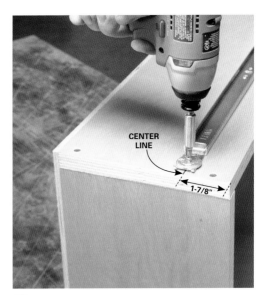

8 Build the drawer frame and measure for drawers. Make sure your drawers fit perfectly by building the drawer frame first. Then measure between the slides and build your drawers to exactly this width.

9 Mount the drawer slides. Draw a line parallel to the top of the drawer to indicate the center of the drawer slide. Line up the slide by centering the line in screw holes. Attach the slide with the screws provided.

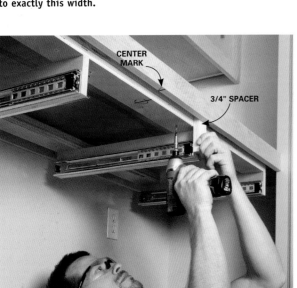

10 Hang the frame under the countertop. Make center marks on the frame and the underside of the counter and align them. Then use a spacer to set the frame 3/4 in. back from the countertop edging and drive the screws.

11 Glue on the drawer front. Starting with the center drawer front, dab on hot-melt glue and press it against the drawer. Quickly center the drawer front 1/4 in. below the countertop edge. Hold it still for about 10 seconds until the glue cools. Now position the other two drawer fronts. Drive screws from the inside.

are not very forgiving, so measure and attach the drawer dividers carefully so the dividers are perfectly parallel when the frame is assembled.

For our 24-in.-deep countertop, we used 20-in. drawer slides. We cut the drawer dividers (K) 20 in. long and built the drawer boxes 20 in. deep. If your closet is shallower, use shorter slides and adjust these dimensions to match. The drawer slides have two parts. One mounts to the dividers and the other to the drawer. Remove the part that attaches to the drawer according to the included

instructions. Then screw the part of the slide with the ball bearings to the dividers, aligning the bottom edges. The center dividers will have drawer slides on both sides. Screw through the stringers (J) into the drawer dividers (K) to build the frame. Be careful to keep the front of the drawer slides facing forward. Then add the second layer of stringers (J). Check the frame against a framing square as you screw it together to make sure it's square. When the frame is complete, measure between the slides to determine the drawer sizes (Photo 8).

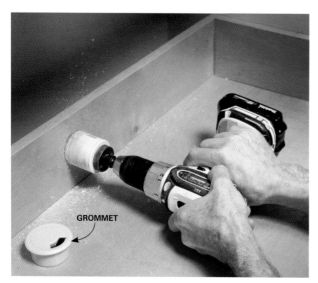

GROMMET

12 Hide cords behind a tall backsplash. Attach the backsplash with cleats, holding it about 4 in. from the wall. Then drill holes where you'll have cords and install cord grommets.

Build the drawers by screwing through the sides into the fronts and backs, and then gluing and nailing on the plywood bottom. Nail one edge of the bottom to the drawer box. Then use a framing square to square the drawer box before nailing the other three edges. To attach the drawer slide to the drawers, we first drew lines 1-7/8 in. down from the top edges of the drawers (Photo 9). (You may have to adjust this distance to match your drawer slides. The dimension isn't critical as long as there's about a 1/4-in. clearance between the drawer and the stringer when the drawer is mounted.) Then sight through the screw holes in the slides to center them on the line before attaching them with the included screws.

Finish the drawer installation by attaching the frame to the underside of the countertop (Photo 10) and installing the fronts. Hold the drawer frame back 3/4 in. from the back of the countertop edging. Install the drawers by lining up the slides and pushing them in. Photo 11 shows a tip for aligning the drawer fronts. The hot-melt glue holds the fronts temporarily. Attach them permanently by opening the drawers and driving four 1-1/4-in. screws through the drawer box into the drawer front from the inside.

Finish it off with a cord-concealing backsplash

Here's a handy method to hide cords and still have easy access to them. Simply mount a backsplash board about 4 in. from the back wall to create a cord trough. Figure B shows how we used a cleat to attach the backsplash. Drill holes through the face and install cord grommets to allow cords to pass through. We found 2-in. cord grommets at the home center, but since they were a loose fit in the 2-in. hole, we held them in place with a dab of silicone caulk. Lay a multi-outlet power strip behind the backsplash for extra outlets. We drilled a hole through the countertop so that we could plug the power strip into a wall outlet. You can also nail backsplash boards to the end walls for a more finished look.

The outlet, reinvented

The standard outlet worked great for a hundred years with only a few changes. But in the age of portable devices, it needed a complete redesign. The reinvented outlet has one standard receptacle for old-fashioned needs and two ports for high-tech gizmos. Just plug in your USB cable and walk away. A smart chip inside the outlet adjusts output to suit your device, so there's no need for the wall-wart adapter that came with the device. The maximum output is 2.1 amps—that's enough to charge two phones or one tablet. And of course, you can always plug an adapter into the old-fashioned receptacle to charge a third device. The Leviton T5630 is one brand. It installs like a standard outlet and is sold at home centers.

Technology tips

Get the right part

The appliance (auto, plumbing, computer) parts store always seems to ask for the one piece of information you didn't write down. So shoot a photo of the entire appliance nameplate and take it with you. Sure, you can do that with any camera phone. But can you read the numbers on that tiny 2-in. screen? Nope. A smartphone screen is much larger and lets you zoom in to read smaller information. It works great for paint labels too—saves the trouble of dragging paint cans to the store.

Bad memory? There's an app for that

Use an app for your smartphone to help you organize jobs into labeled and colored notes (The Color Note app for Android phones is shown here, but there are similar apps for the iPhone). Anytime you need to remember something like spark plug sizes, belt sizes, dimensions, furnace filter sizes, air filters, etc., enter it into your phone. You can also take pictures of a disassembly so you can put the item back together again without any leftover parts. This also helps when you're shopping since you have all the info and pictures with you all the time.

Binder-clip cable catcher

If you haven't run across this particular cable-organizing tip yet, it's time you did, because it's dirt simple and pure genius. Clamp a binder clip to the edge of your desk to holster USB cables. No more cables slipping behind your desk into the dusty darkness below.

I.D. cables with bread tags

The little plastic tags used to close bread bags are handy for identifying the cables on your computer components. Just write the name of the device on the tag and slip it around the cable. No more wondering which cable belongs to which device.

BREAD BAG TAG

TIP:
It's important to keep computer components at least 6 in. away from magnets

Magnetic office supplies holder

Here's a perfect way to organize all those paper clips, rubber bands and pushpins. All it takes is a magnetic knife/tool holder strip, small jars with lids and a few fender washers. (The strips are sold at bath stores, hardware stores, home centers and online retailers.) You don't even need the fender washers if you buy jars with steel lids that will stick to the magnet on their own.

Clamp the magnetic strips to the underside of a shelf or cabinet. Drill pilot holes and screw the strip into place (Photo 1). If the jars have steel lids, fill them with office supplies and stick them up on the magnetic strip. If the jar lids are aluminum or plastic, use cyanoacrylate glue (Super Glue is one brand) to attach a fender washer to the top of each lid (Photo 2). After they dry, fill the jars, stick them up on the magnet and think about some other project to do instead of the work waiting for you on your desk.

1 Clamp the magnetic strip in place, drill pilot holes and drive in the screws that come with the strips.

FENDER WASHER

2 Glue fender washers to plastic or aluminum jar lids so they'll stick to the magnetic strip. Skip this step if your jars have steel lids.

Label-palooza!

O ne downside of having stuff is finding what you need, when you need it. Constantly searching for something not only wastes time, but it can drive you bonkers! Labeling can help. Here are a slew of smart and creative labeling tips from our readers and Field Editors.

Label-maker mania

There should be a 12-step program for people who become addicted to their label makers. It starts when you innocently label tool cabinet drawers. Do the power strip next, and suddenly you just can't stop. The confusing light switches in the entryway—labeled. The kitchen items you take to potluck dinners—labeled with full names. File folders, the fuse box, pantry jars, tools the neighbors borrow, power adapters—stop before you label again!

Instant labels for parts drawers

Plastic drawers let you see the nails or screws inside, but you can't always tell their size. Here's a simple solution: Cut the labels off fastener boxes and tape them inside the front of each drawer. You'll know exactly where everything is located at a glance.

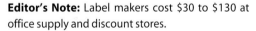

CHILI POWDER PARSLEY RED PEPPER MUSTARD

LAMP POST   PORCH   HALL

Editor's Note: Label makers cost $30 to $130 at office supply and discount stores.

Color-coded wrenches

Reader photo

Use colored vinyl tape on your wrenches to identify the type. Wrap a strip of blue tape around the handle of metric wrenches and red tape around the SAEs. Don't cover the whole handle, just a strip of tape once around at one end so you don't cover up the size marking.

Chalkboard paint

Chalkboard paint is great for creating reusable labels on metal bins, jars, drawers and a ton of other things. When you change the contents of a drawer or jar, you just wipe off the chalk and rewrite the label.

Chalkboard paint is available in spray-on and brush-on versions at home centers and hardware stores.

You can apply chalkboard paint directly to most non-porous surfaces. Or make your own adhesive and magnetic labels by covering mailing labels and refrigerator magnets with chalkboard paint.

Printable magnetic labels

If you have terrible handwriting, try making magnetic labels with a home printer. Just create the labels on your computer, put the magnet sheets in your printer, hit "print" and cut them up. They're great on metal file drawers and tool chests. When you reorganize, just move the labels around or add new ones.

Editor's Note: Avery Magnet Sheets, which are compatible with ink-jet printers, are available in five-sheet packs at office supply stores and online retailers.

Chalkboard sticky labels

You can also buy already-painted self-adhesive labels at amazon.com and other online retailers. Search for "chalkboard stickers."

SELF-ADHESIVE LABELS

Tough labels for soft bags

If you carry around soft-sided bags like camping duffels, sports bags and tool cases, you'll want labels that stand up to being squashed, mashed, soaked, yanked, dropped and rolled around. They can be tough to find, but a good solution is nylon webbing (found at camping and fabric stores) or short lengths of tie-down straps. Just tie the webbing around the handle of your bag and label it using a waterproof marker.

Headache remedy

Whenever you buy child-protected bottles of aspirin or ibuprofen, color both of the white arrows with red fingernail polish. That way, when you need some medicine, you can immediately see how the arrows line up and get the cap off fast.

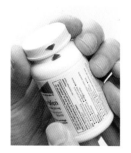

Bin index

A lot of people love large plastic bins. But remembering what's inside each bin is tough, and reading a small label is nearly impossible when your bins are stored high on garage shelves. Solve both problems by labeling your bins with large numbers. Each number corresponds to a page in a binder that lists the contents of each bin. It's simple to change the list, and it's a heck of a lot easier to find what you need by checking the binder than by rummaging through each bin.

Editor's Note: When it comes to bin I.D. tags, you can also try adhesive storage pouches that let you slip index cards in and out easily. You can find these at office supply stores or online retailers.

Reader photo

Self-stick vinyl labels

Self-adhesive vinyl letters make great labels indoors and out. You can get them at office supply stores, art stores and online retailers. Some versions are reflective and perfect for dark areas such as basements and the garage. Use them inside the kitchen cabinets to remind kids to put things back where they got them!

Emergency labels

Label all the important switches and valves around the house with shipping labels. These include the main water shutoffs and the well electric switch. Then take photos of all the shutoffs with the tags attached and put them in a "House Reference" binder. If there's a leak when you're not home, everyone will know what to do to prevent a disaster.

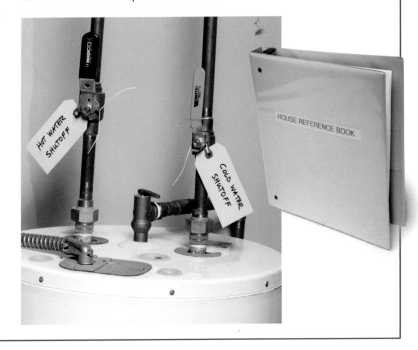

◄── PLASTIC STENCILS

Stencil smarts

An old-school labeling technique is to use plastic stencils (available at art and office supply stores) and spray-paint your name and address on things that have a tendency to "walk" away. Stencil trash cans, sleds, tool cases and recycling bins. If your children don't stop wandering away, stencil them too!

WHAT IT TAKES

Time: 2 hours
Skill level: Intermediate

Add home office outlets

S urface wiring is a system of channels and boxes that allow outlets, switches or light fixtures to be put anywhere—without the hassle of cutting into walls, fishing wire and patching holes. And it can look much less messy, since the parts can be painted to match the walls. Mount outlets low on walls where they'll be hidden by furniture.

All the parts are available in metal or plastic at home centers. This project uses plastic because it is easier to cut. All it takes for the project is wire, connectors, outlets and cover plates.

Add outlets to an existing circuit unless a device that draws a lot of power, such as an air conditioner or a space heater, will be plugged in to the same circuit. An electrical inspector will review the plan before approving a permit. Be sure to have the work inspected when it's complete.

Start by mounting a box base at an existing outlet (Photo 1). Cut out the back panel of the box with a utility knife before screwing it to the junction box. Then use a stud finder to locate studs and mark them with masking tape.

Run the channel to the first outlet location (Photo 2). If the channel won't have to make any turns or run around corners, just cut it to length with a hacksaw. But if the channel turns up or down or goes around a corner, miter the adjoining ends at a 45-degree angle. To mount the channel base, drill 1/8-in. holes at each stud and 1/2 in. from the ends. Wherever an end doesn't land on a stud, use a drywall anchor.

With the first section of channel in place, fasten a box base to the wall. Don't cut out the back panel. If the base lands on a stud, simply screw it to the stud. If not, use two drywall anchors. Continue adding channel and boxes.

Next, run wire from the existing junction box to each box base. The size of the wire added must match the size of the existing wire. Use the labeled notches on a wire stripper to check the gauge of the existing wire (14-gauge is most common, but it may have 12-gauge wire). Use only individual wires labeled "THHN," which is sold in spools or by the foot at home centers and hardware stores. Get three colors: green for the ground, white for the neutral, and red or black for the hot wire. Don't simply buy plastic-sheathed cable and run it inside the channel.

Cut channel covers to length (no need to miter them). At turns or corners, hold an elbow in place when measuring for the covers—the elbow will overlap about 1/4 in. of the cover.

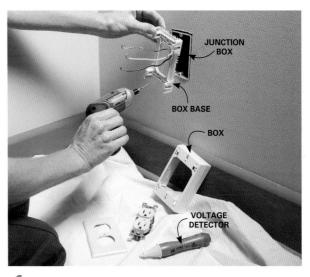

JUNCTION BOX

BOX BASE

BOX

VOLTAGE DETECTOR

1 Turn off the power and make sure it's off using a voltage detector. Remove the old outlet and screw a box base to the junction box.

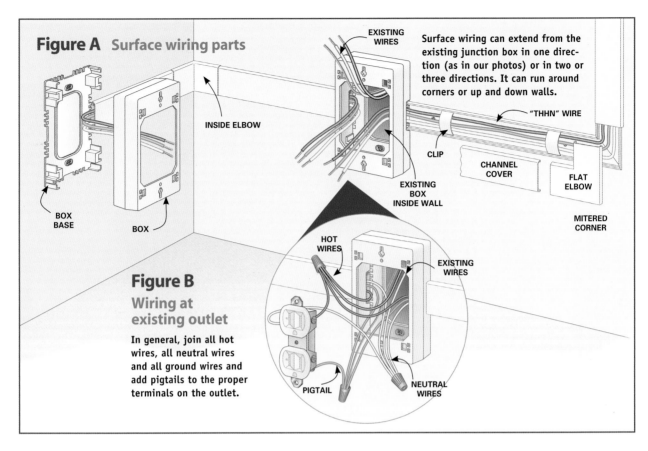

Figure A Surface wiring parts

BOX BASE

BOX

INSIDE ELBOW

EXISTING WIRES

Surface wiring can extend from the existing junction box in one direction (as in our photos) or in two or three directions. It can run around corners or up and down walls.

"THHN" WIRE

CLIP

CHANNEL COVER

FLAT ELBOW

MITERED CORNER

EXISTING BOX INSIDE WALL

Figure B
Wiring at existing outlet

In general, join all hot wires, all neutral wires and all ground wires and add pigtails to the proper terminals on the outlet.

HOT WIRES

EXISTING WIRES

PIGTAIL

NEUTRAL WIRES

Snap the covers onto the channel base followed by the elbows and boxes (Photo 3). Wiring the outlets is similar, whether several outlets are added or only one. If two channels run from the existing junction box (as in Figure A), there will be two new sets of wire to connect to the old wiring (Figure B). If channel runs only one direction from the box (as in these photos), there will be fewer wires, but the process is the same: Join all the hot wires together, all the neutrals together and all the grounds together. Wiring is similar at the new outlet boxes that fall between sections of channel (Photo 3 shows "pigtails" ready for an outlet). At the last box in the run, there will be only three wires (see Figure A); connect them directly to the new outlet.

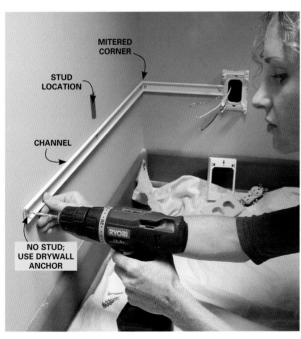

MITERED CORNER

STUD LOCATION

CHANNEL

NO STUD; USE DRYWALL ANCHOR

2 Cut the channel to length, drill holes and screw it to studs. If the ends don't land on studs, fasten them with drywall anchors.

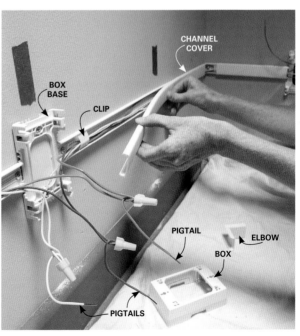

CHANNEL COVER

BOX BASE

CLIP

PIGTAIL

ELBOW

BOX

PIGTAILS

3 Mount a box base on the wall. Run wire and secure it with clips. Snap the cover and elbows over the channel. Then snap the boxes onto the bases. Add outlets.

Bedroom, closet & entryway

Small-closet organizer

Most bedroom closets suffer from lack of organization—stuff on the floor; a long, overloaded closet rod; and a precariously stacked, sagging shelf. The simple shelving system shown here cleans up that clutter. It provides a home for shoes; several cubbies for loose clothing, folded shirts, sweaters or small items; and a deeper (16-in.-wide) top shelf to house the stuff that keeps falling off the narrow shelf. Besides the storage space it provides, the center tower stiffens the shelf above it as well as the clothes rod, since it uses two shorter rods rather than a long one.

You can cut and assemble this entire shelving system from a single sheet of plywood (for a 6-ft.-wide closet). Birch plywood is used because it's relatively inexpensive yet takes a nice finish. The edges are faced with 1x2 maple for strength and a more attractive appearance. The bottom shelves roll out for easier access.

The key tool for this project is a circular saw with a cutting guide for cutting the plywood into nice straight pieces (Photo 1). An air-powered brad nailer or finish nailer makes the assembly go much faster, and a miter saw helps produce clean cuts. But neither is absolutely necessary.

Cut the birch plywood to size

Rip the plywood into three 15-3/4-in. by 8-ft. pieces (Photo 1), then cut the sides and shelves from these with a shorter cutting guide. For an average-size closet—6 ft. wide with a 5-1/2-ft.-high top shelf—cut all the sides and shelves from one piece of

BEFORE **AFTER**

3/4-in. plywood. Making the shelving wider means settling for fewer shelves/trays or buying additional plywood. Be sure to support the plywood so the pieces won't fall after completing a cut, and use a guide to keep the cuts perfectly straight. Use a plywood blade in a circular saw to minimize splintering. Cut slowly on the crosscuts, and make sure the good side of the plywood is down—the plywood blade makes a big difference, but the thin veneer will splinter if you rush the cut.

Mark and cut the baseboard profile on the plywood sides, using a profile gauge (Photo 2) or a trim scrap to transfer the shape, or remove the baseboard rather than cutting the plywood and reinstalling it later. Either method works fine.

1/2" PARTICLE-BOARD GUIDE

A

B

A

E

E

C

D

E

D

2x4 SUPPORTS

BEST SIDE FACING DOWN

1 Cut the sheet of plywood into three equal widths using a saw guide. Then crosscut the sections into the pieces shown in Figure A, p. 44, using a shorter guide.

Figure A Small-closet organizer

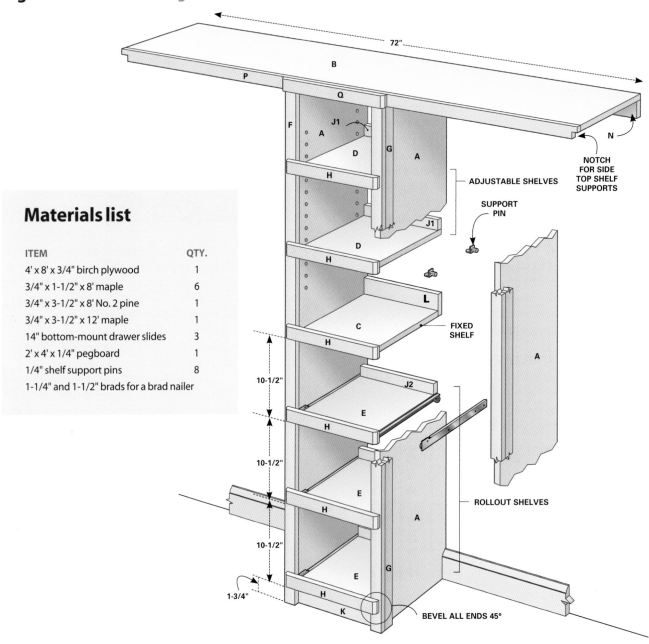

72"

B

P

Q

J1

F

A

D

G

A

H

NOTCH
FOR SIDE
TOP SHELF
SUPPORTS

N

ADJUSTABLE SHELVES

SUPPORT
PIN

J1

D

H

L

C

FIXED
SHELF

A

H

J2

E

10-1/2"

H

E

10-1/2"

ROLLOUT SHELVES

H

A

E

G

10-1/2"

E

1-3/4"

H

K

BEVEL ALL ENDS 45°

Materials list

ITEM	QTY.
4' x 8' x 3/4" birch plywood	1
3/4" x 1-1/2" x 8' maple	6
3/4" x 3-1/2" x 8' No. 2 pine	1
3/4" x 3-1/2" x 12' maple	1
14" bottom-mount drawer slides	3
2' x 4' x 1/4" pegboard	1
1/4" shelf support pins	8
1-1/4" and 1-1/2" brads for a brad nailer	

Cutting list

KEY	PCS.	SIZE & DESCRIPTION
A	2	15-3/4" x 65-1/4" plywood (sides)
B	1	15-3/4" x 72" plywood (top shelf)
C	1	15-3/4" x 12" plywood (fixed shelf)
D	2	15-3/4" x 11-7/8" plywood (adjustable shelves)
E	3	15-3/4" x 11" plywood (rollout shelves)
F	2	3/4" x 1-1/2" x 64-1/2" maple (vertical front trim)
G	2	3/4" x 1-1/2" x 65-1/4" maple (vertical side trim)
H	6	3/4" x 1-1/2" x 14-1/2" maple (shelf fronts)

KEY	PCS.	SIZE & DESCRIPTION
J1	2	3/4" x 1-1/2" x 11-7/8" maple (shelf backs)
J2	3	3/4" x 1-1/2" x 11" maple (rollout shelf backs)
K	1	3/4" x 1-1/2" x 12" maple (base)
L	5	3/4" x 3-1/2" x 12" pine (bracing)
M	2	3/4" x 3-1/2" x 24" maple (side top shelf supports—not shown)
N	2	3/4" x 3-1/2" x 29-1/4" maple (rear top shelf supports)
P	1	3/4" x 1-1/2" x 72" maple (top shelf edge)
Q	1	3/4" x 1-1/2" x 15-3/4" maple (top trim)

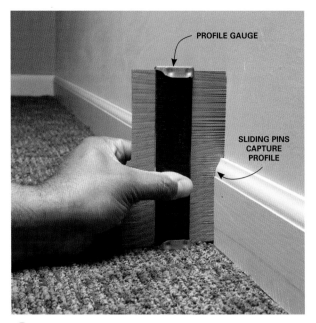

2 Make an outline of the baseboard with a profile gauge and, using a jigsaw, cut out the pattern on the lower back side of the two shelving sides. (See Figure A and Photo 4.)

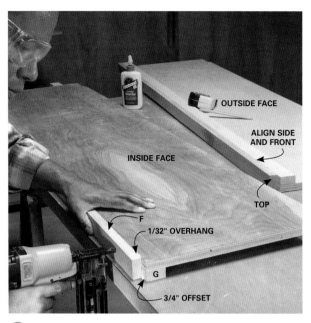

3 Cut the 1x2s to length. Then glue and nail them to the plywood sides (Figure A) with 1-1/4-in. brads. Note the slight (1/32-in.) overhang along the inside.

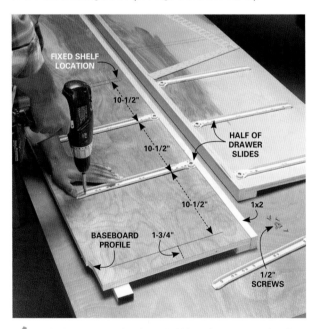

4 Mark the center and rollout shelf locations using a framing square. Then mount half of each of the two-piece drawer slides even with the 1x2 on each side.

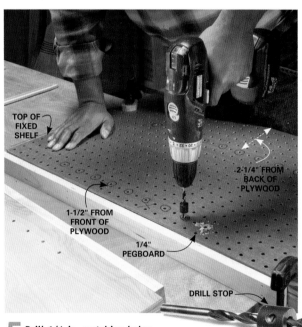

5 Drill 1/4-in. matching holes 3/8 in. deep for the adjustable shelf pins using a pegboard template. Flip the pegboard when switching sides.

Attach the maple edges

Glue and nail the side 1x2s (G) to the best-looking side of the plywood (so it faces out), holding them flush with the front edge (Photo 3). Be sure to use 1-1/4-in. brads here so the nails don't go completely through the side. Use 1-1/2-in. brads everywhere else.

> **TIP:**
> Hold the brad nailer perpendicular to the grain whenever possible so the rectangular nailheads will run with the grain instead of cutting across it. This makes them less prominent.

Then attach the front 1x2s (F). These 1x2s should be flush with the bottom of the sides, but 3/4 in. short of the top. The 1x2s will overlap the edge slightly because 3/4-in. plywood is slightly less than a full 3/4 in. thick. Keep the overlap to the inside.

Lay out the locations for the drawer slides and the fixed center shelf before assembling the cabinet—the 12-in. width is a tight fit for a drill. Use the dimensions in Photo 4 and Figure A for spacing. Vary any of these measurements to better fit shoes or other items. Then take the drawer slides apart and mount them on the tower sides (Photo 4). Remember that one

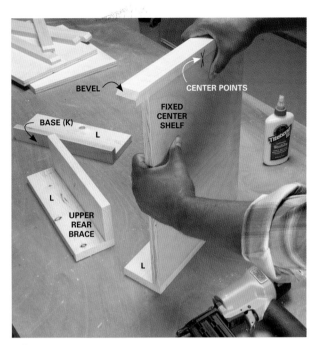

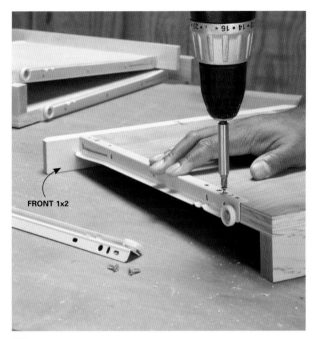

6 Assemble the shelves and shelving braces using glue and 1-1/2-in. brads. Align the centers of each piece for accurate positioning.

7 Attach the other halves of the slides to the rollout shelves with 1/2-in. screws. Butt them against the front 1x2.

side of each pair is a mirror image of the other.

To position the shelf support pins for the two adjustable shelves, align the bottom of the 1/4-in. pegboard with the fixed shelf location, then drill mirror-image holes on the two sides (Photo 5). Mark the holes to be used on the peg-

> **TIP:**
> Make sure the pegboard has square sides.

board—it's all too easy to lose track when flipping the pegboard over to the second side. Use a brad point drill bit to prevent splintering, and place a bit stop or a piece of tape for a 5/8-in. hole depth (1/4-in. pegboard plus 3/8 in. deep in the plywood). Most support pins require a 1/4-in.-diameter hole, but measure to make sure.

Cut the bevels and assemble the shelves

Cut the bevels in all the 1x2 shelf fronts, then glue and nail them to the plywood shelves, keeping the bottoms flush (Photo 6). Nail 1x2 backs (J1 and J2) onto the adjustable and rollout shelves. Next, nail together the bracing (L) and the base piece (K), which join the cabinet. Then add the slides to the rollout shelves (Photo 7).

Assembling the shelving tower is straightforward (Photo 8). Position the L-shaped bracing at the top and braces at the bottom, add glue to the joints, then clamp and nail. Because of the slight lip where the 1x2 front trim (F) overlaps the plywood, it requires chiseling out a 1/32-in.-deep x 3/4-in.-wide notch so the fixed shelf will fit tightly (Photo 9).

Set the cabinet in the closet

Remove the old closet shelving and position the new cabinet. If there's carpeting, it's best to cut it out under the cabinet for easier carpet replacement in the future (Photo 10). For the cleanest

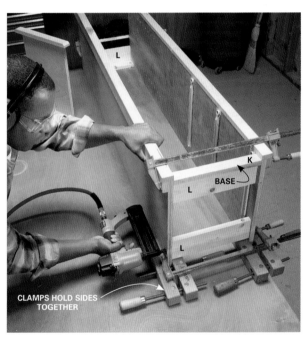

8 Set the sides on edge, glue and clamp the braces (L) in place and nail the assembly together with 1-1/2-in. brads. Make sure the braces are square to the sides.

look, pull the carpet back from the closet wall, cut out the padding and tack strip that fall under the cabinet, and nail new tack strips around the cabinet position. Then reposition the cabinet, push the carpet back against it and cut the carpet. Or, simply cut out the carpet and tack strip under the cabinet and tack the loose carpet edges to the floor (but it won't look as nice).

Plumb and level the cabinet, then screw it to the wall. Use hollow wall anchors if the studs are hard to find. The cabinet will be firmly anchored by the upper shelf anyway.

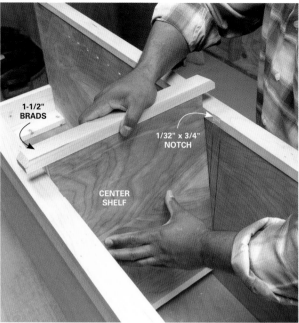

9 Chisel shallow slots in the 1x2 overhang, then slide the center shelf into place. Nail at the front, back and sides.

1-1/2" BRADS

1/32" x 3/4" NOTCH

CENTER SHELF

10 Center the cabinet in the closet against the back wall, mark its position and cut the carpet out around it. Tack the loose edges of carpet to the floor.

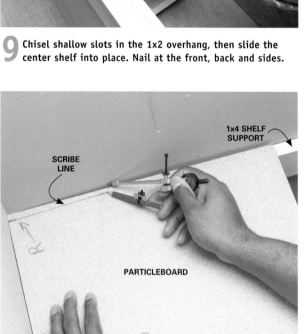

11 Shove a 16 x 24-in. sheet of particleboard into the shelf corners and scribe a line. Cut along the scribe line and use the particleboard as a pattern. Nail the shelf to the supports and cabinet top.

1x4 SHELF SUPPORT

SCRIBE LINE

PARTICLEBOARD

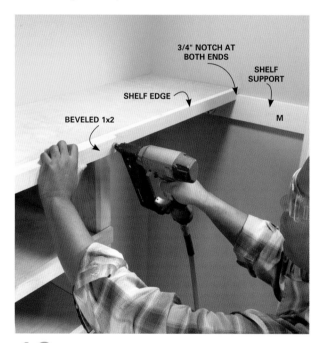

12 Notch the 1x2 shelf edge over the end supports and nail it into place. Then trim the top of the cabinet with a beveled 1x2.

3/4" NOTCH AT BOTH ENDS

SHELF SUPPORT

SHELF EDGE

BEVELED 1x2

M

Scribe the top shelf for a tight fit

Closet shelves are tough to fit because the corners of the walls are rarely square. To cut the shelf accurately, scribe a leftover 16-in.-wide piece of particleboard or plywood in both corners (Photo 11) and use it for a template for cutting the ends of the shelf. Then the shelf will drop right into place and rest on 1x4 supports nailed to the side walls and back wall. Make sure the front of the shelf is flush with the front of the tower and nail it to the top. If the back wall is wavy, scribe the back of the shelf to the wall and trim it to make the front flush. Then cut and notch the front 1x2 and nail it to the shelf (Photo 12).

Lightly sand all the wood and apply a clear finish. When it's dry, mix several shades of putty to get an exact match to your wood and fill the nail holes. Add another coat of finish and let it dry. Screw on the clothes rod brackets, aligning them with the bottom of the 1x4. Then pile on the clothes.

Traditional coat & mitten rack

WHAT IT TAKES

Time: 1 day
Skill level: Intermediate

This coat rack is easy to build with butt joints connected by screws that get hidden with wooden screw-hole buttons and wood plugs. It mounts easily to the wall with screws driven through the hidden hanging strip on the back. The five large Shaker pegs are great for holding hats, umbrellas and coats, and the hinged-hatch door at the top keeps the clutter of gloves and scarves from view.

Maple is an ideal wood for Shaker-style pieces, but any hardwood will do. All you need for this project is wood, hardware and varnish.

Cutting the pieces

First transfer the pattern measurements in Figure A, p. 49 (using a compass), and then cut the sides (A) with a jigsaw. Next cut the top (D) to length and rip the shelf (B) to the width given in the Cutting List, p. 49. Cut the hanging strip (F) and the peg strip (C) to the same length as the shelf (B). Now drill the 3/8-in.

counterbore holes for the screw-hole buttons (with your spade bit) 3/16 in. deep into the outsides of parts A (as shown in Figure A, and Photo 2). Also drill the 3/8-in. counterbore holes in the top. These holes must be 3/8 in. deep.

Mark and drill the 1/2-in. holes for the Shaker pegs in the peg strip. Drill the holes for the Shaker pegs perfectly perpendicular to the peg strip to ensure they all project evenly when glued in place.

NOTE:
Be sure this project is screwed to the wall studs. Drill two holes into the hanging strip at stud locations and use 2-1/2-in. or longer wood screws.

Figure A
Coat & mitten rack details

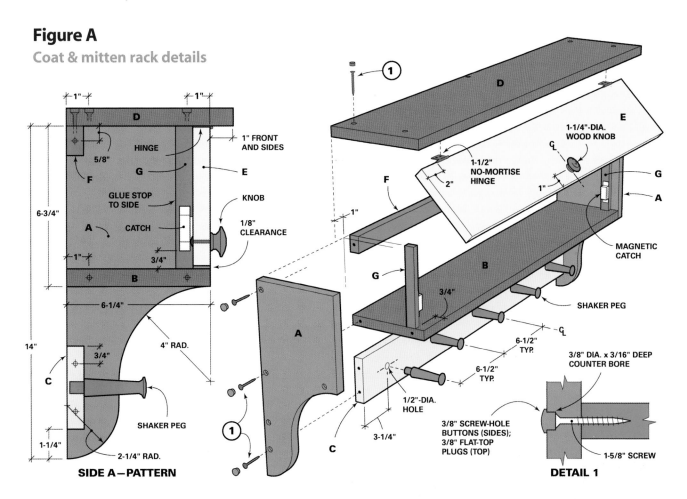

SIDE A — PATTERN

1" FRONT AND SIDES
1" front and sides
HINGE
5/8"
6-3/4"
GLUE STOP TO SIDE
CATCH
A
B
6-1/4"
14"
3/4"
4" RAD.
C
SHAKER PEG
1-1/4"
2-1/4" RAD.
F
G
E
KNOB
1/8" CLEARANCE
3/4"

1-1/2" NO-MORTISE HINGE
2"
1-1/4"-DIA. WOOD KNOB
1"
F
G
A
E
MAGNETIC CATCH
B
3/4"
SHAKER PEG
6-1/2" TYP.
6-1/2" TYP.
1/2"-DIA. HOLE
3-1/4"
C
3/8" SCREW-HOLE BUTTONS (SIDES); 3/8" FLAT-TOP PLUGS (TOP)

DETAIL 1

3/8" DIA. x 3/16" DEEP COUNTER BORE
1-5/8" SCREW

Cutting list

KEY	PCS.	SIZE & DESCRIPTION
A	2	3/4" x 6-1/4" x 14" maple sides
B	1	3/4" x 6-1/4" x 32-1/2" maple shelf
C	1	3/4" x 3-1/2" x 32-1/2" maple peg strip
D	1	3/" x 7-1/4" x 36" maple top
E	1	3/4" x 5-13/16" x 32-5/16" maple hatch
F	1	3/4" x 1-1/4" x 32-1/2" maple hanging strip
G	2	3/4" x 1/2" x 6" maple hatch stop

Materials list

ITEM	QTY.
1-1/2" no-mortise hinges	1 pair
1-1/4" beech knob	1
Narrow magnetic catch	2
3-3/8"-long Shaker pegs	5
3/8" screw-hole buttons	10
3/8" plugs	5
3/8" spade bit	1
1/2" spade bit	1
1-5/8" wood screws	15
Wood glue	1 pint
Wipe-on polyurethane	1 pint
150- and 220-grit sandpaper	

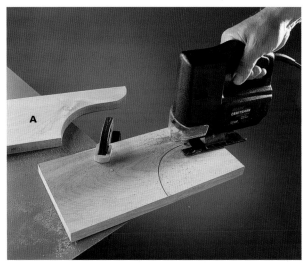

1 Cut the side pieces (A) using a jigsaw or band saw. Sand the curved edges smooth.

Assembly

Lay the pieces on your workbench, as shown in Photo 3. Align the hanging strip (F), the shelf (B) and the peg strip (C) as shown and clamp the sides (A) to these parts. Predrill the holes with a combination pilot hole/countersink bit using the center of the counterbore holes as a guide. Next, screw the sides to B, C and F. Fasten the top (D) to the sides in the same manner. Glue and clamp the hatch stops to the insides of parts A, as shown in Figure A. To finish the assembly, cut the hatch (E) to size and install the hinges to the underside of part D and the top of the hatch. Now glue the buttons and pegs into their corresponding holes. Use only a small drop of glue for the buttons but be sure to apply a thin layer of glue completely around the plugs. This will swell the plugs for a tight fit.

Finishing

Lightly sand the entire piece after assembly with 220-grit sandpaper. Apply two coats of clear wipe-on polyurethane to all the surfaces (remove the hinges and knobs). Once the finish is dry, add two magnetic catches to the hatch-stop molding (G).

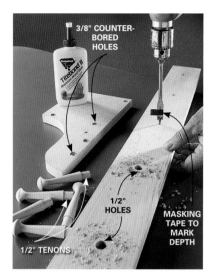

2 Drill the 1/2-in. holes 5/8 in. deep for the 3-3/8-in. Shaker pegs. Drill the 3/8-in. counterbore holes 3/16 in. deep for the screw-hole buttons in the sides (see Figure A, Detail 1).

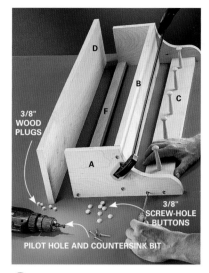

3 Assemble the shelf by clamping parts C, F and B to the sides. Drill pilot holes and screw the pieces together. The screws will be covered by the buttons and plugs.

Super stuff sacks

Ever try, unsuccessfully, to fit 10 lbs. of blankets into a 5-lb. bag? Now you can do it with ease. Space-saving storage bags use a vacuum cleaner to ensure that you're only storing stuff, not air.

If you put lots of winter clothes and bedding in storage every spring, then spend the summer trying to stop the bulky winter stuff from tumbling out of closets and drawers, you'll like these bags. Just fill the bag with clothes or bedding, seal the top, and pull the air out using a vacuum. Seal the vacuum port and you're good to go. The bags can be reused, so come fall you can store your summer stuff.

No matter how you put items into the bag, the vacuum suction will compress them. However, the more neatly you fill the bag, the flatter it will end up. Various sizes are available, so you can match the size to the items you're storing. Several brands of these bags are sold at big-box stores and online.

BEFORE

AFTER

Coat & hat rack

Organize your hallway or mudroom with this simple, attractive coat and hat rack. You just cut the boards to fit your space, paint them, outfit them with different kinds of hooks to suit your needs and then screw them to the wall. Shown are 6-ft.-long 1x4s, but use whatever length works for you and the space available. Shown is poplar, which is the best choice if you want a painted finish. If you're after a natural wood look, choose any species you want.

Finish the boards first and then attach your hooks. Shown here are drawer pulls down the middle and a robe hook near the top to hold backpacks and larger items. You'll find hooks in a tremendous range of styles, colors and prices at hardware stores and online retailers.

Attach the boards to studs, or to the drywall with screw-in drywall anchors. Drive three screws in each board: one at the top, one in the middle and one at the bottom.

WHAT IT TAKES

Time: 1 hour
Skill level: Beginner

MASKING TAPE FOR LAYOUT

FINISH WASHER

PROTRUDING TIP

2-1/2" SCREW

1 Drive your screws partway into each board so the screw tips poke out the back. Place the boards where you want them, and press hard to mark the spots for your drywall anchors.

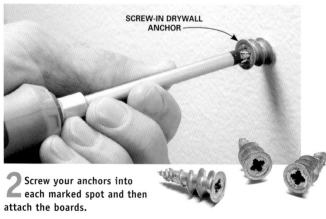

SCREW-IN DRYWALL ANCHOR

2 Screw your anchors into each marked spot and then attach the boards.

Triple your closet space!

If you have to dig through a mountain of clothes to find your favorite sweatshirt, it's time to take on that messy closet. This simple-to-build system organizes your closet with shelf, drawer and hanging space for your clothes, shoes and accessories. Buying a closet system like this would cost you at least $500, but you can build this one for about half that.

This system is really just four plywood boxes outfitted with shelf standards, closet rods or drawers. Here it is built for an 8-ft.-wide closet with an 8-ft. ceiling, but it'll work in any reach-in closet that's at least 6 ft. wide if you adjust the shelf width between the boxes or change the box dimensions.

Three times the storage— and more!

Three times the storage in the same space may sound impossible, but just look at the numbers

Storage Space Comparison for 8-ft. Closet

Before ▉ After ▉

	Before	After
SHELVES	8 FT.	28 FT.
DRAWERS	0	4
CLOTHES ROD	8 FT.	8 FT.
BASKET	0	1

PAINT PAD

SPACER

REFERENCE

1 Finish now, save time later. Prefinishing gives you a faster, neater finish because you'll have fewer corners to mess with. Apply two coats of polyurethane quickly and smoothly with a disposable paint pad.

2 Preinstall drawer slides. Attaching slides is a lot easier before the boxes are assembled. Position the slides using reference lines and a spacer. Remember that there are left- and right-hand slides, usually marked "CL" and "CR."

Time, money and materials

You can complete this project in a weekend. Spend Saturday cutting the lumber, ironing on the edge banding and applying the finish. Use your Saturday date night to clean everything out of the closet. That leaves you Sunday to build and install the new system.

This entire system was built with birch plywood. The cost, including the hardware for the drawers, shelves and closet rods, was around $300 (see Materials List). You could use MDF or oak plywood instead of birch. Everything you need for this project is available at home centers.

Cut and prefinish the parts

Start by cutting all the parts to size following Figure C on p. 57 and the Cutting List on p. 54. The corner box sides are slightly narrower than 12 in., so you can cut off dings and dents and still cut four sides from a sheet of plywood.

You won't be able to cut the shelves that fit between the boxes to length until the boxes are installed (the shelves need to be cut to fit), but you can rip plywood to 11-7/8 in. and cut the shelves to length later.

Once the parts are cut, apply edge banding (iron-on veneer) to all the edges that will be exposed after the boxes are assembled (Figure A). Build a jig to hold the parts upright. Place a part in the jig. Then cut the edge banding so it overhangs each end of the plywood by 1/2 in. Run an iron (on the cotton setting) slowly over the edge banding. Then press a scrap piece of wood over the edge banding to make sure it's fully adhered. Trim the edges with a veneer edge trimmer. Visit familyhandyman.com and search for "edge banding" for instructions.

Lightly sand the wood and your closet rod with 120-grit sandpaper. Wipe away the dust with a tack cloth, then use a paint pad to apply a coat of polyurethane on everything except the drawer parts (Photo 1). This inexpensive pad will let you finish each part in about 20 seconds. Let the finish dry, then apply a second coat.

Attach the hardware

It's easier to install the drawer slides and the shelf standards that go inside the boxes before you assemble the boxes. Use a framing square to draw reference lines on the drawer unit sides for your drawer slides (see Figure A). The slides are spaced 8 in. apart, centered 8-3/4 in. down from the top of the box. Keep the slides 3/4 in. from the front edge (this is where the drawer faces will go). Use a 7/64-in. self-centering drill bit to drill pilot holes and screw the slides into place (Photo 2).

You'll need your wire basket now (available at home cen-

Figure A
Closet storage system

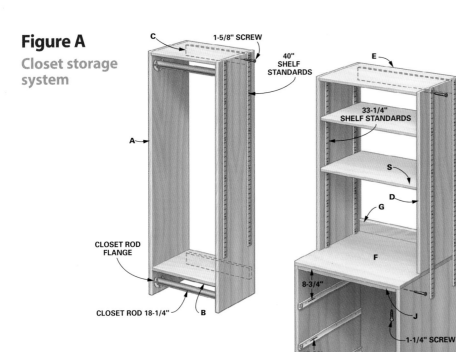

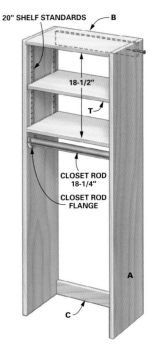

C — 1-5/8" SCREW

40" SHELF STANDARDS

33-1/4" SHELF STANDARDS

A

S

D

G

F

CLOSET ROD FLANGE

CLOSET ROD 18-1/4"

B

8-3/4"

8" ON CENTER

J

1-1/4" SCREW

K

H

L

WIRE BASKET

13"

45° ANGLE

20" SHELF STANDARDS

B

18-1/2"

T

CLOSET ROD 18-1/4"

CLOSET ROD FLANGE

A

C

Figure B   Drawer construction

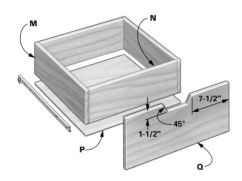

M

N

7-1/2"

45°

1-1/2"

P

Q

Materials list

ITEM	QTY.
4' x 8' x 3/4" plywood	3
4' x 8' x 1/2" plywood	1
4' x 8' x 1/4" plywood	1
8' closet rod	1
Edge banding (iron-on veneer)	2 pkgs.
20" drawer slides	4 prs.
6' shelf standards	10
Closet rod flanges	10
Wire basket	1
2-1/2" screws	1 box
1-5/8" trim screws	1 box
1-1/4" screws	1 box
1" screws	1 box
Wipe-on poly	1 pint

Cutting list

KEY	PCS.	SIZE & DESCRIPTION
A	4	3/4" x 11-7/8" x 52" corner box sides
B	4	3/4" x 11-7/8" x 18-1/2" corner box tops and bottom
C	4	3/4" x 2-1/2" x 18-1/2" corner box screw strips
D	2	3/4" x 13-7/8" x 34" shelf unit sides
E	1	3/4" x 13-7/8" x 22-1/2" shelf unit top
F	1	3/4" x 21" x 24" shelf unit bottom
G	2	3/4" x 2-1/2" x 22-1/2" shelf unit screw strips
H	2	3/4" x 20-3/4" x 44" drawer unit sides
J	1	3/4" x 20-3/4" x 22-1/2" drawer unit top
K	1	1/4" x 24" x 44" drawer unit back
L	1	3/4" x 2" x 22-1/2" drawer unit cleat
M	8	1/2" x 6" x 19" drawer sides
N	8	1/2" x 6" x 20" drawer fronts and backs
P	4	1/4" x 20" x 19" drawer bottoms
Q	4	3/4" x 7-3/4" x 22-1/4" drawer face
R	8	3/4" x 11-7/8" adjustable shelves, cut to length (not shown)
S	2	3/4" x 13-7/8" x 22" adjustable shelves for shelf unit
T	1	3/4" x 11-7/8" x 18" right corner box adjustable shelf
U	1	3/4" x 14-1/4" x 96" top shelf (not shown)

3 Gang-cut the standards. Cutting 16 standards one by one with a hacksaw would take hours. Instead, bundle two or more together with tape and cut them with a jigsaw.

SHELF STANDARDS

METAL BLADE

4 Nail first, then screw. If you have a brad nailer, tack the boxes together to hold the parts in position. Then add screws for strength.

ters). Attach the glides for the basket 3 in. below the drawer slides. If your basket is narrower than 22-1/2 in., screw a cleat to the box side so the basket will fit.

Now attach the shelf standards. You can cut them with a hacksaw, but an easier way is to use a metal blade in a jigsaw. Place two or more standards together so the numbers are oriented the same way and the standards are aligned at the ends. Tape the standards together where you're going to make the cut, then gang-cut them with your jigsaw (Photo 3).

Screw the standards to the inside of the box sides, 1 in. from the edges. Keep the standards 3/4 in. from the top (that's where the box tops go). Be sure the numbers on the standards are facing the same way when you install them—this ensures the shelves will be level.

Assemble the boxes

Use a brad nailer to tack the boxes together following Figure A and Photo 4. If you don't have a brad nailer, use clamps. Then screw the boxes together. Use 1-5/8-in. trim screws because the screw heads are small and unobtrusive (you can leave the screw heads exposed). Here are some tips for assembling the boxes:

■ Attach the screw strips to the box tops first, then add one side, then the bottom shelf, and then the second side.

■ Drill 1/8-in. pilot holes to prevent splitting. Stay 1 in. from edges.

■ If your cuts are slightly off and the top, bottom and sides aren't exactly the same width, align the front edges.

■ The boxes will be slightly wobbly until they're installed in the closet, so handle them with care.

■ The middle bottom box has a back. Square the box with the back, then glue and tack the back in place.

■ After the corner boxes are assembled, screw shelf standards to the side that doesn't abut the wall (it's easier to install the standards before the boxes are installed).

Build the drawers

Cut the drawer sides and bottoms (see Cutting List, p. 54). Assemble the sides with glue and 1-in. screws. To square the drawers, set adjacent sides against a framing square that's clamped to your work surface. Glue and tack the drawer bottom into place (Photo 5). Then set the drawer slides on the drawers, drill pilot holes and screw the slides into place.

5 Square the drawer boxes. If the boxes aren't square, the drawers won't fit right or glide smoothly. Drawers take a beating, so assemble them with nails and glue.

6 Center the drawer faces perfectly. Stick the faces to the boxes with double-sided tape. Then pull out the drawer and drive screws from inside the box.

7 Plumb the shelf boxes. The corners of your closet may not be plumb, so check the box with a level before you screw it to the studs. Mark stud locations with masking tape.

8 Install the center unit in two parts. The center unit is big and clumsy, so install the shelf unit first, then prop up the drawer unit with spacers and screw it to the shelf.

Install the drawers in the box. Getting the drawer faces in their perfect position is tricky business. If the faces are even slightly off-center, the drawer won't close properly. To align them, place double-sided tape over the drawer front. Starting with the top drawer, center the drawer face in the opening (Photo 6). You should have about a 1/8-in. gap on both sides and the top. Press the face into the tape. Take out the drawer and clamp the face to the drawer to keep it stationary. Drive two 1-in. screws through the inside of the drawer into the face.

Hang the boxes in the closet

Now install the boxes. Start by drawing a level line in the closet, 11 in. down from the ceiling. This will give you just over 10 in. of storage space above the closet system after the top shelf is installed. Then mark the stud locations on the wall with tape.

Don't assume your closet walls are plumb—they're probably not. So you can't just place a box in a corner without checking for alignment. Hanging the boxes is a two-person job, so get a helper. Start with the corner boxes. Align the top of the box with your level line on the wall. Have your helper plumb the box with a level while you drive 2-1/2-in. screws through the screw strip into the wall at the stud locations (Photo 7). Attach the other corner box the same way.

Find the center of the wall, then make a mark 12 in. on one side of the center mark. That's where your shelf unit will go. Again, have your helper plumb the box while you align it with your marks and screw it to the wall.

Prop up the drawer unit on spacers so it's tight against the shelf unit. Align the edges, then clamp the boxes and screw them together (Photo 8). Drive screws through the screw strip into the wall.

Then place the top shelf over the boxes. This shelf barely fit into place. If yours won't fit, you'll have to cut it and install it as two pieces. Make the cut near one end, over a corner box, so it's not noticeable. Screw the shelf to the box tops with 1-1/4-in. screws.

Then attach shelf standards along the sides of the shelf and drawer units (Figure A). Cut the adjustable shelves to length to fit between the corner boxes and the middle boxes. Finally, screw the closet rod flanges into place, cut the closet rod to size and install the rods.

Figure C
Closet system cutting diagrams

This shows only the 3/4-in. plywood. The 1/2-in. and 1/4-in. plywood sheets are for the drawers and back.

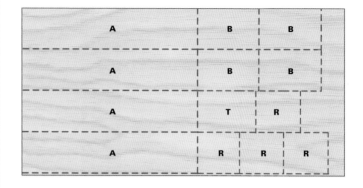

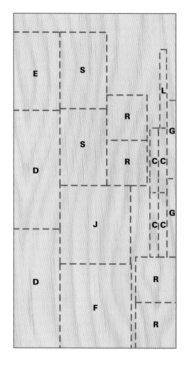

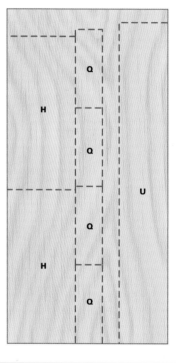

Entry organizer

Sturdy cubbies, hooks and shelves contain the clutter

the sides, nailing from inside with 1-1/4-in. brad nails so the nails are hidden. Set the sides upright on a large worktable or flat area of the floor, then nail the top, bottom and center fixed shelves to the nailers. Keep the best edges of the sides facing up. Check to be sure all the edges are aligned to each other in the front as you assemble the locker.

After the shelves are nailed into place, square the locker by measuring diagonally from corner to corner, first from one side and then the other, and then pushing the corners in or out until the measurements are equal. Set the two center dividers into place, square them against the front edge, and then nail them through the top and bottom fixed shelves, using four nails at each end.

Turn the locker over so the back is facing up. Measure the location of the center dividers and shelves from the sides, then mark these locations on the back of the plywood. Set the plywood on the back of the locker with the best side facing down. Predrill and screw the plywood down at one corner, then align the rest of the framework to the plywood as you screw it down to the sides. Finally, screw the plywood to the center dividers and shelves. Use four screws for each divider and shelf and eight for each side.

Turn the locker over again and glue and nail the back shelf supports to the plywood, tight up against each shelf. Fasten the nailers to the plywood with 1-1/4-in. nails, but drive them at about a 15-degree angle so they don't stick through the back of the plywood. You may also need to lower the air pressure on your compressor.

Nail the front trim to the front edge of the shelves and to the sides, then glue and nail the front support under the bottom shelf, into the back of the 1x4 base.

Finally, attach the shelf standards and hooks. You can make one cubby all shelves or leave the shelves out entirely

WHAT IT TAKES

Time: 1 day
Skill level: Beginner

Need a home for all the coats, toys, books, shoes and other stuff that accumulates next to your entry door? Adjustable shelves and hooks make this open locker the perfect catchall. Construction is simple—just cut the pieces to length and nail them together. The total cost is several hundred dollars, but you can build it for less if you substitute plywood for the 16-in.-wide laminated pine panels shown here.

First, sand the plywood back and both sides of the pine panels with 120- or 150-grit sandpaper. Check the ends of the panels to make sure they're square and measure the widths to make sure they're all the same. If you want to paint the plywood back and pine panel sides and shelves different colors, as shown, paint or stain all the pieces separately before putting the locker together.

Cut all the panels and shelves to the lengths in the Cutting List. Glue and nail the top, bottom and center nailers to

Cutting list

KEY	PCS.	SIZE & DESCRIPTION
A	2	3/4" x 16" x 7' sides
B	3	3/4" x 16" x 46-1/2" fixed shelves
C	1	48" x 84" x 1/2" plywood back
D	2	3/4" x 16" x 65-1/4" center dividers
E	1	3/4" x 3-1/2" x 48" front trim
F	2	3/4" x 2-1/2" x 48" front trim
G	6	3/4" x 16" x 14-1/2" shelves
H	3	3/4" x 1-1/2" x 45" supports
J	6	3/4" x 1-1/2" x 16" nailers
K	2	3/4" x 1-1/2" x 14-1/4" shelf supports
L	1	3/4" x 1-1/2" x 15" center shelf support

Figure A
Organizer details

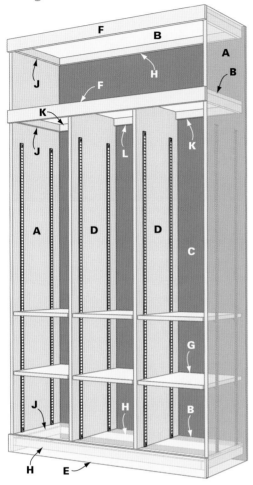

Overall dimensions: 84" H x 48" W x 17-1/4" D

and just make space for hanging coats. Locate and mark the wall studs, then move the locker into position. For a permanent installation, remove the baseboard and recut it around the locker. Shim the base of the locker, if necessary, then screw the locker to the studs just above the center shelf to prevent it from ever tipping forward.

Materials list

ITEM	QTY.
16" x 3/4" x 8' laminated pine panel	6
4' x 8' x 1/2" finish-grade plywood	1
1x2 x 8' pine	3
1x3 x 10' clear pine	1
1x4 x 6' clear pine	1
Shelf standards (5' or 6')	12
1-1/4" screws	1 lb.
1-1/4" brad nails	1 lb.

Storage above windows and doors

The empty wall space above doors and windows is organizational gold! Hang a shelf there and use it for bathroom towels, toiletries, books, files, tablecloths—the list is endless.

Picture-hanging perfection

When you're hanging a group of pictures, it can be hard to visualize exactly where everything should go. Try this next time: Lay them all out on the floor and get them arranged just how you like them. Then flip them over and make a little diagram of your grouping. Measure the distance of each picture's hanger from the adjacent walls, and jot it down on your diagram. Transfer those hanger locations to the wall and you'll have a perfect grouping every time.

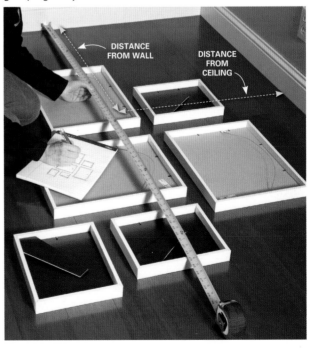

Under-bed rollout

Some of the most useful and under-utilized storage space in your home is right under the bed, and you can take advantage of it with this durable rollout chest, made from a single sheet of plywood. Plastic versions are also available, but wood looks better, lasts longer and lets you custom-size your rollout.

Measure the distance between the floor and the bottom of the bed. Subtract 1/2 in. for clearance under the bed and 1/2 in. (on bare wood) to 1 in. (on thick carpet) for casters. Subtract another 1/2 in. for the hinged top to arrive at the maximum height for the storage box sides.

Mark all the pieces on a sheet of plywood and cut them with a table saw or a circular saw. Fasten 3/4-in. square nailers to the edges of the base with glue and finish nails or screws (1/2-in. plywood is too thin to nail into on edge). Attach the sides to the base, adding square nailers at the corners. Fasten the caster supports to the sides, then nail the outer side pieces to the caster supports.

Attach the front and back. Add the filler strips on top of the caster supports and the last nailer along the top edge of the back. Finally, nail on the fixed top, set the hinged top against it and screw on the hinges. Attach the hinges using 1/2-in. screws so the screws don't stick through the top.

Cutting list

KEY	PCS.	SIZE & DESCRIPTION
A	1	42" x 30-1/2" top
B	2	42" x 6" front and back
C	4	33" x 6" sides
D	1	42" x 4" fixed top
E	1	37" x 33" base
F	2	33" x 3/4" x 3/4" side nailers
G	3	35-1/2" x 3/4" x 3/4" front and back nailers
H	4	4-3/4" x 3/4" x 3/4" corner nailers
J	2	33" x 1-1/2" filler strips
K	4	3-5/8" x 1-1/2" x 5-1/2" caster supports

Note: All 1/2" plywood

WHAT IT TAKES

Time: 2 hours
Skill level: Beginner

Materials list

ITEM	QTY.
AC-grade 4' x 8' x 1/2" plywood	1
3' x 3/4" x 3/4" square dowels	6
2x6 x 2' pine	1
2" fixed caster wheels	4
1-1/2" hinges	4
1" and 1-1/2" brad nails	

Note: All materials and dimensions are for a 7-1/2-in.-tall under-bed space. If you have more or less space, adjust these measurements.

Figure A Rollout construction

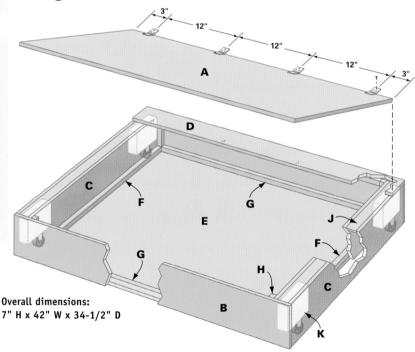

3" 12" 12" 12" 3"

A

D

C

F

G

E

J

G

F

G

H

C

B

K

Overall dimensions:
7" H x 42" W x 34-1/2" D

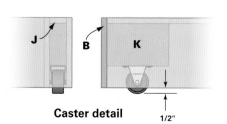

J B K

Caster detail 1/2"

CHAPTER

4

Garage & basement

Upgrades for the garage mechanic

Fixing mechanical contraptions is hard enough without having to mop up the oil, grease and gas that spilled on your workbench or spending half your time looking for tools. We've put together five great garage improvements that'll save you cleanup time and keep your tools in order—all without breaking the bank.

An always-clean workbench

This sheet metal workbench cover is easy to clean (just squeegee the oil into the gutter and drain bucket), and it's heavy-duty enough to handle heavy car parts. All it takes is some measuring and sketching and a trip to a sheet metal shop or a local HVAC shop and steel yard. The whole thing assembles in less than an hour and costs less than $300.

Skip the steel decking if you wish, but it does prevent the top from denting and provides a more solid work surface. You can cut the 11-gauge (1/8-in.) steel plate into thirds for easy transport.

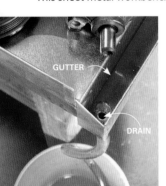

GUTTER

DRAIN

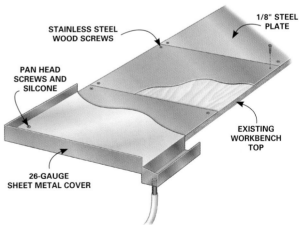

STAINLESS STEEL
WOOD SCREWS

1/8" STEEL
PLATE

PAN HEAD
SCREWS AND
SILCONE

EXISTING
WORKBENCH
TOP

26-GAUGE
SHEET METAL COVER

Drill, countersink and screw the steel plate to any wood top. Then screw down the cover with a few pan head screws covered with a dollop of silicone. Clamp a vinyl tube onto the drainpipe and route it into a bucket.

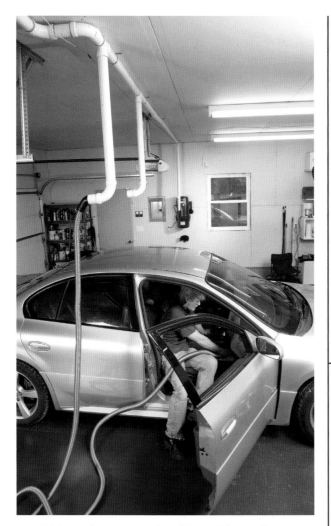

Jack and jack-stand holder

Haven't you tripped over your jack stands enough? Build this brain-dead-simple storage rack and get them off the floor. If you have a lightweight floor jack, add mounting hooks under the holder. Screw a 2-in. PVC coupler onto the side of the rack and a 2-in. cap on the wall near the floor for the handle.

Install 2-in. sanitary tees on the ceiling and drop a pipe near each car door. Install a long 90-degree bend and a stubout to connect the hose. Cap off the stubout with a standard 2-in. pipe cap when not in use.

Central vac for the garage

OK, this setup is overkill. But once you get a wall-mounted wet/dry vacuum mounted to the wall, it just makes sense to run inexpensive 2-in. PVC all over the place. That way you don't have to drag a 35-ft. hose all over the garage. Buy adapters to connect standard plumbing PVC to the vacuum (central vacuum fittings are 2-in. O.D., while plumbing fittings are 2-in. I.D.).

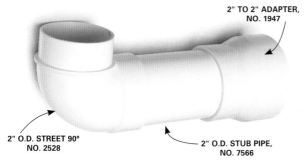

2" TO 2" ADAPTER, NO. 1947

2" O.D. STREET 90° NO. 2528

2" O.D. STUB PIPE, NO. 7566

Connect the plumbing pipe to the power unit with adapter fittings. Search "central vacuum stores" online for parts.

PVC drawer organizers

When you're right in the middle of a project, you don't need to waste time pawing through drawers looking for tools. So keep frequently used tools neatly stacked in your workbench drawer using this handy setup.

Cut 1- or 2-in. PVC pipe to length. Glue on end caps and then slit each pipe in half on a band saw. Screw them to the drawer bottoms and load them up!

Grease gun holster

A grease gun is big and, uh, greasy. So don't slime up your drawers or cabinets with it. Slice up a few sections of 1-in. and 3-in. PVC pipe and screw them to a plywood backer to make this slick grease gun holder. Then slap up a 2-in. coupler and cap to hold a back-up tube of grease.

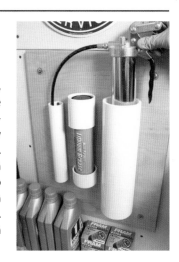

Flexible garage storage

WHAT IT TAKES

Time: 1 day
Skill level: Beginner

Squeeze more stuff into less space!

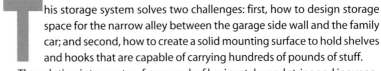

This storage system solves two challenges: first, how to design storage space for the narrow alley between the garage side wall and the family car; and second, how to create a solid mounting surface to hold shelves and hooks that are capable of carrying hundreds of pounds of stuff.

The solution is to create a framework of horizontal wood strips and inexpensive shelf standards. It can hold almost any arrangement of shelving and hooks, at any point on the wall, and it's easy to rearrange.

Planning and materials

Pull your car into the garage and measure how much space is available. Then look over what you need to store and figure out where it will fit. Generally it's best to hang narrow shelves and smaller hooks lower where space is tight, with wider shelves up near the ceiling so you don't bump your head or interfere with car doors.

Planning the layout and buying materials can take a few hours, but you can do the actual installation, including ripping the plywood shelves and strips, in less than a day. Put up horizontal strips even if you have exposed studs or block walls—they'll make it much easier to install shelf standards and hooks. Apply finish to the strips and shelves, if desired, before installing them.

We used 3-1/2-in.-wide strips of 3/4-in. plywood for the strips because plywood is always straight and never splits—but pine 1x4s also work. Birch plywood was our choice for the strips and shelves, but you can also use less-expensive BC plywood. You can rip 12 strips from one 4 x 8-ft. sheet— that's enough for an average wall. (If you don't have a table saw, go to familyhandyman.com and search for "circular saw" for tips on making straight cuts.) We used four sheets of plywood for our system. For shelf edging, we used 1-1/2-in.-wide strips of solid birch (Photo 6). The total cost for our 20-ft.-long system was about $500, but you could cut that cost in half by skipping the fold-down workbench (Photo 5) and using less-expensive wood and plywood.

Just screw wood strips to the wall

Strips of plywood fastened horizontally to the studs are the key to this system. Once they're up, you can easily mount any kind of storage hardware or shelf standard without worrying about where the stud is or whether a drywall anchor will hold. Since you can drive a screw anywhere, you can pack more stuff on the wall.

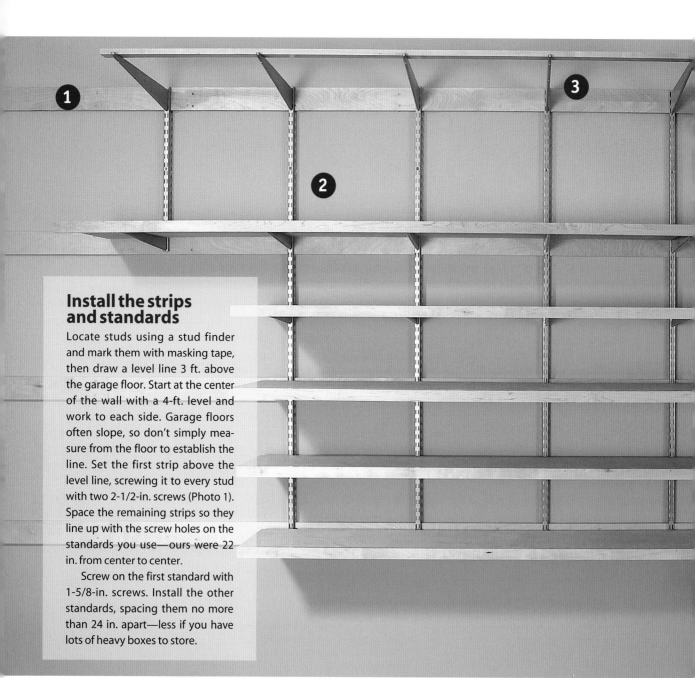

Install the strips and standards

Locate studs using a stud finder and mark them with masking tape, then draw a level line 3 ft. above the garage floor. Start at the center of the wall with a 4-ft. level and work to each side. Garage floors often slope, so don't simply measure from the floor to establish the line. Set the first strip above the level line, screwing it to every stud with two 2-1/2-in. screws (Photo 1). Space the remaining strips so they line up with the screw holes on the standards you use—ours were 22 in. from center to center.

Screw on the first standard with 1-5/8-in. screws. Install the other standards, spacing them no more than 24 in. apart—less if you have lots of heavy boxes to store.

STUD

EXTRA HAND

ALIGN WITH SCREW HOLES IN STANDARDS

1 Screw plywood strips to the studs. Cut them to length so the ends meet on the studs.

24" MAX.

STANDARD

2 Mount the first shelf standard, then use it as a reference to locate the others. Space standards no more than 24 in. apart.

3 Lock brackets together with a wood lip to create a lumber and pipe rack. The lip keeps pipes and lumber from falling off.

Customize the system to fit your needs

Attach pegboard, different widths and lengths of shelving, a workbench, a lumber and pipe rack, and any other type of storage you need (Photos 3 – 5).

Use a table saw or circular saw to rip shelving 1/2 in. wider than the depth of the shelf bracket. Use 3/4-in.-thick plywood or solid wood for the shelves—it's stronger and resists sagging better than any particleboard shelving product available.

If you want to make the shelves more rigid as well as more attractive, nail on 1x2 front edges (Photo 6). Use an air nailer or predrill if hand nailing. Finally, line up the shelves and attach them to the brackets from underneath with screws 1/2 in. longer than the depth of the bracket.

4 Add a section of pegboard. Frame the edges with wood strips and fasten all four sides of the pegboard.

5 Mount heavy-duty folding brackets on a 3/4-in. plywood backer to create a fold-down workbench.

PLYWOOD BACKER

FOLDING BRACKET

6 Apply a bead of wood glue to each shelf edge, then nail on edging with finish nails every 12 in.

Tips for the garage

Tight-space garage storage

If your garage is too narrow for most shelving systems, here's a great way to store a lot of stuff in very little space. Hang several multilevel wire racks on the wall—the same racks you use in a pantry. They hold a ton and hug the wall, so they don't get in the way.

Garage extension cord reel

Tired of digging out your extension cord every time you want to use it in the garage? Try this easy tip: Attach a retractable cord reel to your garage ceiling and plug your cord into the unused outlet mounted near your garage door opener. Your cord will always be centrally located and easily accessible, yet out of the way when you're not using it.

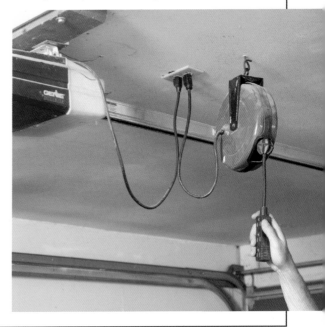

Brilliant bungee cord storage

Bungee cords always seem to end up in a tangled mess. To keep them organized, screw a scrap piece of closet shelving to the wall and hook the cords along its length. It'll be easy to find the one you need.

Mark Hardy

Storage tips

Holiday light storage stands

Storing dozens of holiday light strings each year without wrecking them is tough, but this method may be a winner. Just screw a dowel to each end of a wooden base cut to the size of a large plastic bin. Then wrap your lights around the dowels in a figure eight and place the stand in the bin. You'll be amazed how many light strings you can wrap around the stands without tangles or damage.

Soft stuff

Extra-large Ziploc bags (sold at home centers and online) are great for storing comforters, patio cushions and out-of-season clothes. Here's a slick trick for getting all the air out of the bag before you seal it. Put your items inside and push out all the air you can by hand. Then seal the bag but leave an opening large enough to fit a drinking straw. Use the straw to suck out the remaining air and then finish sealing the bag.

Skinny laundry room cart

A lot of laundry rooms have a narrow wasted space either next to or between the washing machine and dryer, and it's usually a hideout for socks and lint. To take advantage of this space, build a simple plywood cart on fixed casters to hold detergents and other laundry supplies.

Ornaments by the cup

It's hard to store fragile ornaments without breaking them. That's the beauty of this solution: Use a plastic storage container and store each ornament in a separate plastic cup. By using cardboard to separate the layers, you can stack a lot of ornaments in one sturdy box without any tangling or breaking. You can reuse the same cups and cardboard year after year.

PLASTIC CUP

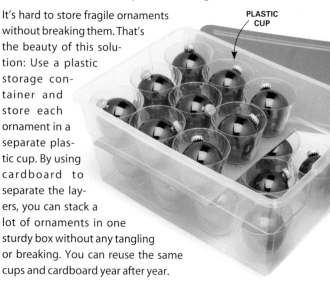

Simple utility cabinets

Build 'em and fill 'em. These sturdy cabinets are designed for simple assembly. Just glue and screw plywood together to make the basic box, then add a premade door—actually an inexpensive bifold door panel. Since bifolds are readily available in several styles, including louvered and paneled, it's easy to make a wide range of practical yet handsome cabinets without the time and hassle of making the doors.

Make the cabinets big and deep to store clothing and sports gear; shallow and tall for shovels, rakes, skis or fishing rods; or shallow and short to mount on walls for tools, paint cans and other small items. Or mount them on wheels and roll the tools right to the job. The only limitation is the size of standard bifold doors.

Here you'll learn how to build one of the smaller hanging wall cabinets. Use the same techniques and the Cutting Lists on pp. 71 and 74 to build others.

Advanced skills or special tools are not needed to build this entire set of cabinets. However, it does require cutting a lot of plywood accurately. A table saw helps here, but a circular saw with a guide works fine too. Add a drill or two, a couple of clamps and some careful advance planning, and start building!

Buying the bifolds and plywood

When planning the cabinets, begin by choosing the bifold door and build the rest of the cabinet to match its dimensions. Standard bifolds are 79 in. high and available in 24-in., 30-in., 32-in.

and 36-in. widths. Keep in mind that it takes two doors for each of these widths, each approximately 12, 15, 16 or 18 in. wide. The cabinet can be any of the single-door widths or any of the double-door widths. Or cut the doors down to make shorter cabinets, as demonstrated here. Make them any depth desired.

Bifolds come in several styles and wood species. This project shows louvered pine doors and birch plywood for a handsome, natural look. You can cut the cost considerably by using less expensive plywood, bifolds and hinges.

Also save by using plywood efficiently. Decide on the door sizes, then lay out all the cabinet pieces on a scale drawing of a 4 x 8-ft. sheet of plywood (graph paper helps). Feel free to adjust the cabinet depths a bit to achieve best use. The five cabinets shown were built from four sheets of 3/4-in. plywood and two sheets of 1/4-in. plywood for the backs.

The "partial wrap-around" hinges are available at some home centers or hardware stores. Woodworking stores also carry them (see photo on p. 72). If exposed hinges are OK, simply use bifold hinges, which are available at all home centers.

Cut out all the parts

Begin by cutting the bifold doors to size (Photo 1). This will determine the exact cabinet height. Be sure to use a guide and a sharp blade for a straight, crisp cut. Center the cut on the dividing rail. Be prepared for the saw to bump up and down slightly as it crosses each stile (Photo 1). Then trim each newly created door so that the top and bottom rails are the same width.

TIP:

Most lumberyards and home centers have a large saw (called a panel saw) for cutting sheets of plywood. For a nominal fee, they will rip all of the plywood to proper widths. (Cut the pieces to length later.) It requires planning the cabinet depths in advance, but it's quicker than ripping the plywood at home and makes hauling it a lot easier.

Figure A

Ventilated wall cabinet

TOP (C)

DOOR (BIFOLD CUT OFF) (A)

HANGING CLEAT (E)

11-1/4"

6"

HINGE

MAGNETIC LATCH

FIXED SHELF (D)

CATCH PLATE

SIDE (B)

KNOB

ADJUSTABLE SHELVES (D)

DOOR (BIFOLD CUT OFF) (A)

BACK (F)

HINGE

HANGING CLEAT (E)

43-3/4"

BOTTOM (C)

6"

29-5/8"

Cutting list

KEY	PCS.	SIZE & DESCRIPTION
A	2	14-3/4" x 43-3/4" doors (30" bifold)*
B	2	3/4" x 11-1/4" x 43-3/4" sides
C	2	3/4" x 11-1/4" x 28-1/8" top and bottom
D	3	3/4" x 11-1/4" x 28-1/8" shelves
E	2	3/4" x 3" x 28-1/8" hanging cleats
F	1	1/4" x 29-5/8" x 43-3/4" back

*Exact door sizes vary. Measure the doors before deciding exact cabinet dimensions.

Other cabinet options (Cutting list and dimensions on p. 74)

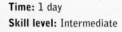

WHAT IT TAKES

Time: 1 day
Skill level: Intermediate

Storage locker

Compact storage for long items like skis, fishing rods and long-handled tools; on the floor or wall-hung; 12-in.-wide door and one fixed shelf.

Closet on wheels

Large storage capacity (about 32 in. wide and 22-1/2 in. deep); fixed shelf; closet rod; 3-in. swivel casters.

Paneled wall cabinet

Shorter version of cabinet above; made from the paneled portion of partial louvered doors; one adjustable shelf.

Narrow floor or wall cabinet

Shelf version of storage locker (left); top and bottom shelves fixed; intermediate shelves mounted on adjustable shelf standards.

1 Mark the door length and clamp a straightedge to the door to guide the saw. Cut the other cabinet pieces using the straightedge as well.

2 Predrill screw holes through the sides 3/8 in. from the ends. Drive 1-5/8-in. screws with finish washers through the sides into the top and bottom. Stack extra shelves in the corners to keep the box square.

Some bifold door manufacturers use only a single dowel to attach each rail to the stile. If that's the case, one of the rails (after being cut in half) is no longer attached to the door. Don't panic. Dab a little glue on each rail and stile and clamp them back together. After 20 minutes or so, they'll be ready.

Then cut the plywood to size using a guide to keep all the cuts straight and square. If the plywood splinters a bit, score the cutting line first with a utility knife.

Assemble the box

Assemble the box face down on a flat surface. The garage floor works well for this step.

Mark and predrill screw holes through the sides for the top and bottom pieces (Photo 2).

This project uses finish washers (available at full-service hardware stores) for a more decorative look.

Attach the fixed shelf next to stiffen and strengthen the box (Photo 3). Use the extra shelves as guides to help position and square the shelf. Predrill and drive three screws through each side into the fixed shelf.

Attach cleats at the top and bottom of the cabinet to use for screwing the cabinet to a wall (Photo 4). Use three or four screws across the top and bottom. Clamp the cleat into place until the screws are driven. Because the screws won't be visible on the top and bottom, skip the finish washers. Make sure the cleat sits flush with the side (Photo 4).

The 1/4-in. plywood back stiffens the frame and keeps it square, which is essential for the doors to fit accurately. Spread glue along the cabinet edges, including the fixed shelf and the hanging cleats (Photo 5). Carefully set the back onto the cabinet, keeping the top flush with the cabinet top. Nail in the order and direction shown in Photo 5. Align the edges carefully before nailing each side to keep the cabinet perfectly square.

Shelves, hinges and other hardware

Use a scrap of pegboard to help lay out the holes evenly for the adjustable shelf support pins. Mark each hole clearly (red circles; see Photo 6) on the front and back of the pegboard. Mark each hole position on one side of the cabinet, then slide the pegboard across to the other side for marking. Don't flip the pegboard over; it can throw the pattern off and the shelves will rock rather than lie flat.

Most shelf support pins require a 1/4-in. hole, but check the pins to be sure. In addition, measure how far the pins are supposed to go into the cabinet sides. Wrap a piece of masking tape around the drill bit at this depth. This ensures that the bit won't go completely through the side of the cabinet. Check the bit after every few holes to make sure the tape hasn't slipped.

Install the door hinges 6 in. from the top and bottom of the doors (add a third hinge on taller doors). The best type is a "partial wrap-around" hinge (Photo 7). Its hinge leaves are hidden when the door is

---

Partial wrap-around hinges

The hinges shown are available at woodworking stores and some hardware stores and home centers.

3 Predrill, clamp and screw the fixed shelf to the sides. Use adjustable shelves as a guide to space it and keep it square.

ADJUSTABLE SHELF

FIXED SHELF

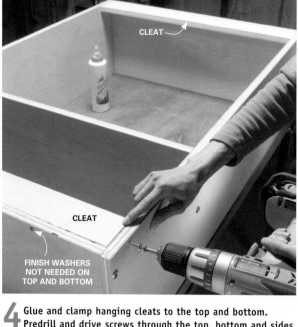

4 Glue and clamp hanging cleats to the top and bottom. Predrill and drive screws through the top, bottom and sides into the cleats.

CLEAT

CLEAT

FINISH WASHERS NOT NEEDED ON TOP AND BOTTOM

5 Spread a bead of glue on all back edges. Then align the plywood back with the top and nail with 1-in. brads. Align the other sides and nail in the order shown.

NAILING PATTERN

CLEAT

FIXED SHELF

6 Mark shelf pin locations on both front and back sides of a pegboard template. Mark one side of the cabinet, then slide (not flip) the pegboard to the opposite side and mark matching holes. Drill the 1/4-in. pin holes.

closed, and the design avoids driving screws into the weak plywood edge grain.

Begin by installing the hinges on the door (Photo 7). Keep them perfectly square to the door edge and predrill screw holes as precisely as possible. An extra set of hands will be helpful when attaching the doors to the cabinet. Have one person align the door exactly with the top or bottom of the cabinet while the second person marks, predrills and screws the hinges to the cabinet side. Repeat for the other door.

Ideally the doors will meet evenly in the center with about a 1/8-in. gap between. If not, "tweak" the hinge positions slightly with paper shims, or plane the doors a bit to make them perfect.

Choose any type of knob and magnetic latch. However, bifold door stiles (the vertical edges) are narrow, so make sure the neighboring door will clear the knob

MASKING TAPE DEPTH GAUGE

Cutting list

Storage locker

KEY	PCS.	SIZE & DESCRIPTION
Door	1	11-3/4" x 79" (half of a 24" bifold)*
Sides	2	3/4" x 11-1/4" x 79"
Top, bottom shelf	3	3/4" x 11-1/4" x 10-1/4"
Cleats	2	3/4" x 3" x 10-1/4"
Front cleat	1	3/4" x 3" x 10-1/4"
Back	1	1/4" x 11-3/4" x 79"

Closet on wheels

KEY	PCS.	SIZE & DESCRIPTION
Doors	2	15-3/4" x 79" (32" bifold)*
Sides	2	3/4" x 22-1/2" x 79"
Top, bottom shelf	3	3/4" x 22-1/2" x 30-1/8"
Cleats	3	3/4" x 3" x 30-1/8"
Back	1	1/4" x 31-5/8" x 79"
Casters	4	3"

Paneled wall cabinet

KEY	PCS.	SIZE & DESCRIPTION
Doors	2	14-3/4" x 32-1/4" (30" bifold)*
Sides	2	3/4" x 11-1/4" x 32-1/4"
Top, bottom shelves	4	3/4" x 11-1/4" x 28-1/8"
Cleats	2	3/4" x 3" x 28-1/8"
Back	1	1/4" x 29-5/8" x 32-1/4"

Narrow floor cabinet

KEY	PCS.	SIZE & DESCRIPTION
Door	1	11-3/4" x 79" (half of a 24" bifold)*
Sides	2	3/4" x 11-1/4" x 79"
Top, bottom shelves	9	3/4" x 11-1/4" x 10-1/4"
Cleats	2	3/4" x 3" x 10-1/4"
Back	1	1/4" x 11-3/4" x 79"

*Exact door sizes vary. Measure doors before deciding cabinet dimensions.

when opened (Photo 8). If there's a rail (the horizontal door frame member), mount the knobs there.

Another potential problem: Bifold stiles are usually 1 to 1-1/8 in. thick and most knobs are designed for 3/4-in. doors. Look for longer knob screws at a local hardware store. Or try this trick: With a 3/8-in. bit, drill a 1/4-in.-deep hole on the back side of the stile to recess the screwhead.

To mount a magnetic latch, first mount the magnet to the underside of the fixed shelf. Stick the catch plate to the magnet with the "mounting points" facing out (photo on right). Close the door and press it tightly against the latch. The points on the catch plate will indent the door slightly and indicate where to mount the plate.

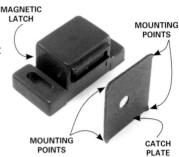

MAGNETIC LATCH

MOUNTING POINTS

MOUNTING POINTS

CATCH PLATE

Finishing

That's about it. These cabinets are finished inside and out with two coats of clear water-based satin polyurethane. It dries quickly (one-half hour), has little or no odor, and cleans up with soap and water. The first coat raises the wood grain a bit, so sand it lightly with fine sandpaper (150 grit or finer). Whether using a clear finish, paint or stain, it's generally faster to remove the doors and hardware first.

6"

7 Screw the hinges to the cabinet doors. Align the door edges with the cabinet top and bottom. Then predrill and screw the hinges to the cabinet sides.

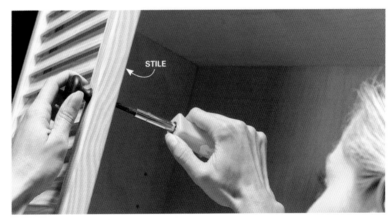

STILE

8 Attach cabinet knobs to the doors and install a pair of magnetic latches to hold the doors closed. For full-length doors, install latches at both the top and the bottom.

Magazine storage bins

Finally got the time to build that project in *The Family Handyman* from three years ago? Great … if you can find the right issue! Here's a handsome solution. Build these bins and stock them with an orderly archive, and you'll have instant access to years of projects and plans. You can build four bins from one 2 x 4-ft. sheet of 1/4-in. plywood and two 6-ft.-long 1x4s. Here's how:

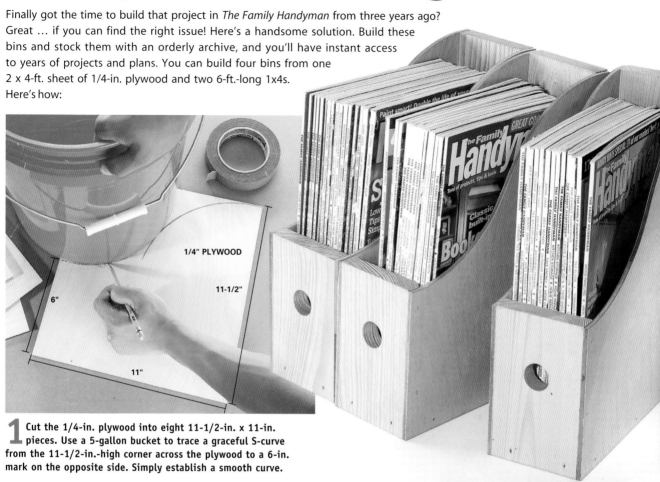

1/4" PLYWOOD

11-1/2"

6"

11"

1 Cut the 1/4-in. plywood into eight 11-1/2-in. x 11-in. pieces. Use a 5-gallon bucket to trace a graceful S-curve from the 11-1/2-in.-high corner across the plywood to a 6-in. mark on the opposite side. Simply establish a smooth curve.

TWO TAPED TOGETHER

2 Stack pairs so the best sides face each other and tape all the sheets together flush at the edges. Gang-cut the curve with a jigsaw or a band saw.

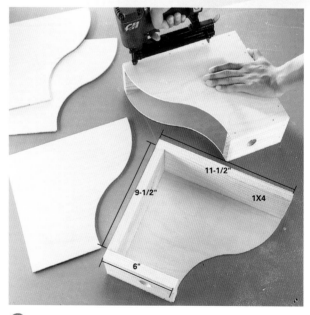

11-1/2"

9-1/2"

1X4

6"

3 Saw pine boards into 6-, 9-1/2- and 11-1/2-in. lengths. Drill 1-in.-diameter finger pulls in the 6-in. pieces, then nail the frames together. Nail the sides to the frames with 1-in. finish nails, sand as needed and apply a finish.

Plywood organizer

Plywood takes up relatively little space and is easy to store—simply lean it against a wall. The trick is getting at it when you need it. Nine times out of 10, you need the half sheet that's buried behind 12 others.

If you've experienced that frustration, you'll love this rack. Casters and a set of hinges are the secret for easy access. They allow you to swing the storage rack out from the wall and slide out the storm window, paneling or other item you want. Dividers strengthen the rack while enabling you to separate large sheets from smaller ones.

Each slot has room for about six sheets of 3/4-in. plywood. Although you can modify this design and make the slots larger, keep in mind that anything that sits around for a year or two is a donation candidate.

WHAT IT TAKES

Time: 2 hours
Skill level: Beginner

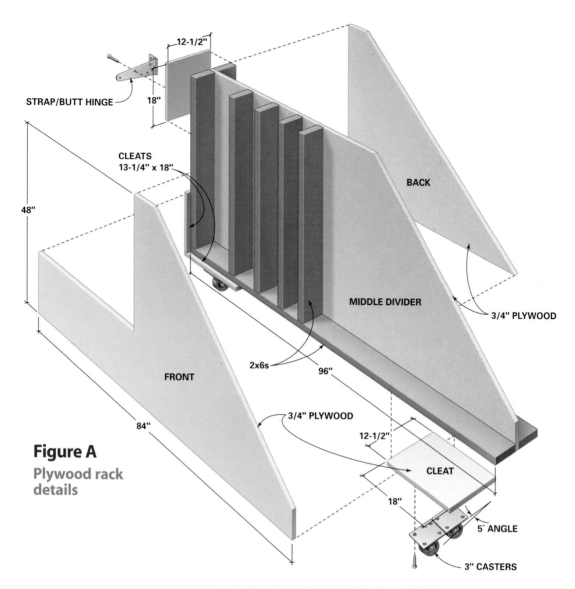

STRAP/BUTT HINGE

12-1/2"

18"

CLEATS
13-1/4" x 18"

48"

BACK

3/4" PLYWOOD

FRONT

MIDDLE DIVIDER

2x6s

96"

3/4" PLYWOOD

84"

12-1/2"

CLEAT

18"

5° ANGLE

3" CASTERS

Figure A
Plywood rack details

Materials list

- Two 4' x 8' sheets of 3/4" AC plywood
- Five 8' construction-grade 2x6s
- Three 3" casters

- One 3" caster with a brake
- 1 lb. of 2" drywall screws
- 1 lb. of 3" drywall screws

- Thirty-four 1/4" x 1-1/2" lag screws
- Two combination 4" butt/ 6" strap hinges (Photo 7)

Figure B: Plywood cutting diagram

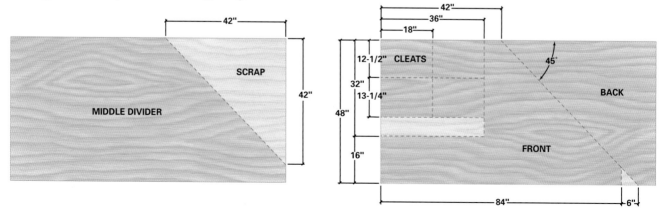

42"

SCRAP

42"

MIDDLE DIVIDER

42"

36"

18"

12-1/2" CLEATS

32"

13-1/4"

48"

16"

45°

BACK

FRONT

84"

6"

1 Cut plywood to the dimensions shown in Figure B. The cuts don't have to be precise; you don't need a saw guide. Wear goggles and hearing protection.

2 Cut the 2x6s to length and position them on the center plywood divider. Tack them to the plywood with 2-in. drywall screws driven from underneath. Then screw the 2x6 dividers to the bottom 2x6 with 3-in. drywall screws.

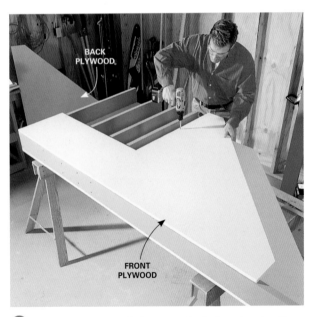

3 Lay the front plywood piece over the 2x6s and anchor it with 2-in. screws driven every 12 inches.

4 Flip the project over and assemble the back section. Position back 2x6s for the bottom and side and fasten them with two 3-in. screws where they meet. Then drive screws at an angle (toe-screw) through the ends of the 2x6s into the assembly below. Attach the plywood back piece to the 2x6s with the 2-in. screws.

Construction of the rack goes surprisingly fast. Plan an afternoon for the project plus an hour or two to run to the home center for materials. (See Materials List on p. 77.) The least expensive wood will do, although for a few dollars more, an AC grade of plywood (sanded on one side) is usually flatter and nicer to work with.

When loaded, this rack is heavy, so make sure to buy casters rated for at least 200 lbs. each. One of the casters should have a brake for extra stability. You can purchase all your materials new, but chances are you'll have some of these materials lying around. (Use up that extra 3/4-in. plywood!)

Cut the plywood and 2x6s to size first, following Figure B, p. 77, for dimensions (Photo 1). You can make your cuts freehand (without a guideboard) because they don't have to be perfect. Use a sharp, carbide-tipped blade with at least 24 teeth to minimize splintering.

After cutting all the pieces, screw the rack together. Start with the center plywood divider first, attaching the bottom

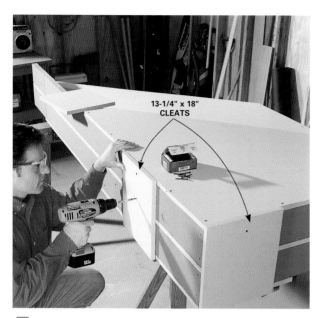

5 Fasten four plywood cleats to the bottom and sides with 2-in. screws to hold the rack together. Use 12 screws per cleat.

13-1/4" x 18" CLEATS

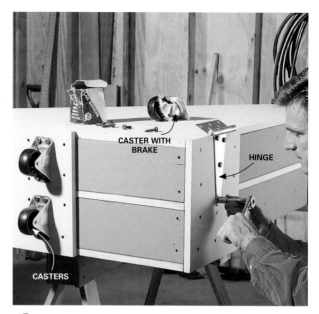

6 Attach the four casters and the strap leaf of the hinges with 1/4-in. x 1-1/2-in. lag screws. Place the caster with a brake on the outer front edge of the rack to hold the rack stationary when sliding items in and out.

CASTER WITH BRAKE

HINGE

CASTERS

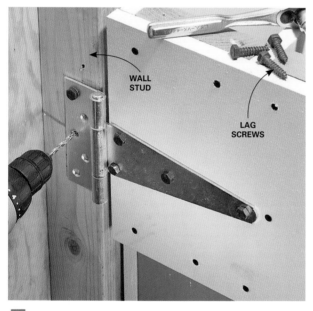

7 Predrill pilot holes and fasten the rack to the wall stud with 1-1/2-in. lag screws.

WALL STUD

LAG SCREWS

8 Swing the rack out from the wall and load it with plywood, drywall and other big, flat stuff.

2x6 and then the side. Use the factory edge of the plywood to keep it all square. Next, measure and mark out your center 2x6 dividers and set them in place (Photo 2). This spacing isn't critical; use more or fewer dividers depending on your needs. After you fasten the front piece of plywood (Photo 3), you can turn the rack over and drive additional screws, spacing them every 12 inches. For the back bin you'll have to toe-screw (screw at an angle) the bottom and side 2x6s through the center plywood divider and into the opposite 2x6 (Photo 4). These toe-screws hold them in place until you attach cleats, which solidly join the two sections (Photo 5).

All that's left is attaching the hardware and fastening the rack to the wall. Since the rack and its contents are heavy, use lag screws to hold the casters and hinges in place. Predrill your holes with a 3/16-in. bit. Set the casters at a slight angle (5 degrees) to accommodate the swing of the rack (Figure A, p. 77). Attach the hinges and you're all set to swing the rack out from the wall and fill it up.

Handy folding table

This 2 x 5-ft. table is a handy option for any laundry room. Located right across from the washer and dryer, it's the perfect place for sorting colors before washing and folding the clothes as soon as they're dry. This project uses heavy-duty brackets that'll hold more than 100 lbs. and neatly fold the top down (preventing future clutter).

Buy the countertop (and end cap) at a home center or salvage one from a friend who's getting new countertops. Also buy three 8-ft. pine boards—a 1x2, a 1x3 and a 1x4—as well as some wood screws. Buy 1-1/4-in. and 2-1/2-in. wood screws for mounting the wall cleats and the countertop stiffeners. Order the fold-away brackets online. (Ours are from rockler.com.)

WHAT IT TAKES
Time: 3 hours
Skill level: Beginner

SHARP BLADE

1 Buy a 6-ft. laminate countertop. Draw a straight line 1-1/2 in. from the back side. Cut this section away with a circular saw. Trim the countertop to length, cutting from the back side.

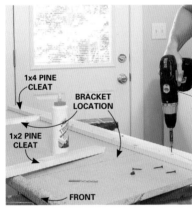

1x4 PINE CLEAT

BRACKET LOCATION

1x2 PINE CLEAT

FRONT

2 Predrill, glue and screw pine supports under the countertop. Use 1x4s along the back and 1x2s at bracket locations. The supports will stiffen the top and provide backing for the brackets. Space the brackets no more than 32 in. apart.

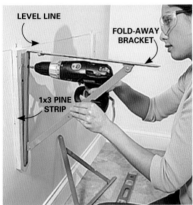

LEVEL LINE

FOLD-AWAY BRACKET

1x3 PINE STRIP

3 Draw a level line 1-1/2 in. below the finished height of the laundry table. This one is 33 in. high including the thickness of the top. Screw 1x3 pine strips to the wall into the studs behind.

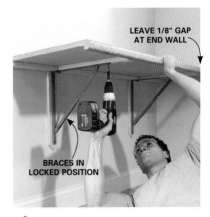

LEAVE 1/8" GAP AT END WALL

BRACES IN LOCKED POSITION

4 Screw the top to the brackets at the pine cleats. Keep about 1/8-in. clearance between the wall and the end for clearance when you lift and close the table. This will prevent damage to the wall.

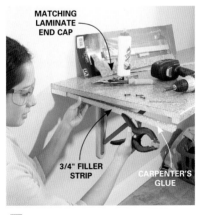

MATCHING LAMINATE END CAP

3/4" FILLER STRIP

CARPENTER'S GLUE

5 Glue and screw the 3/4-in.-thick filler strips to the exposed bottom edge of the counter. Align the filler strip so it's flush with the edge of the top.

6 Trim the laminate end cap with aviator snips to fit the end. Set the iron on medium and slide it across the end panel until the glue bonds. Ease any sharp edges with a metal file.

Outdoor organization & storage

Garden shed

Use it for potting, storage or a small workshop. This light and airy shed does it all.

Don't let the good looks fool you—this 8 x 14-ft. shed has a practical side as well. The bands of windows let in plenty of light and make it a good candidate for a potting shed, an artist's studio or a small workshop. The double doors open wide for easy access to and storage of lawn tractors or other big gardening equipment. And since it's built on a wood platform, you can put it almost anywhere, even on sloping ground or in areas that would be hard to reach with wheelbarrow loads of concrete.

While this isn't a beginner project, if you've built decks or other small structures, you shouldn't have any trouble constructing this shed. The wall and roof framing is straightforward, and the front windows and doors are engineered to be simple to build and install. In this article, we'll show you the basics of how to build the shed and install the windows and doors. For framing, door, window and bracket details as well as a complete materials list, go to familyhandyman.com and enter 58748 into the search box.

Plenty of light for plants or projects

WHAT IT TAKES   **Time:** 3–4 weekends   **Skill level:** Advanced

Continuous bands of windows flood this shed with light and provide great ventilation, making it a bright, airy working space. But if all you need is storage, you can easily build this spacious shed with fewer windows or no windows at all.

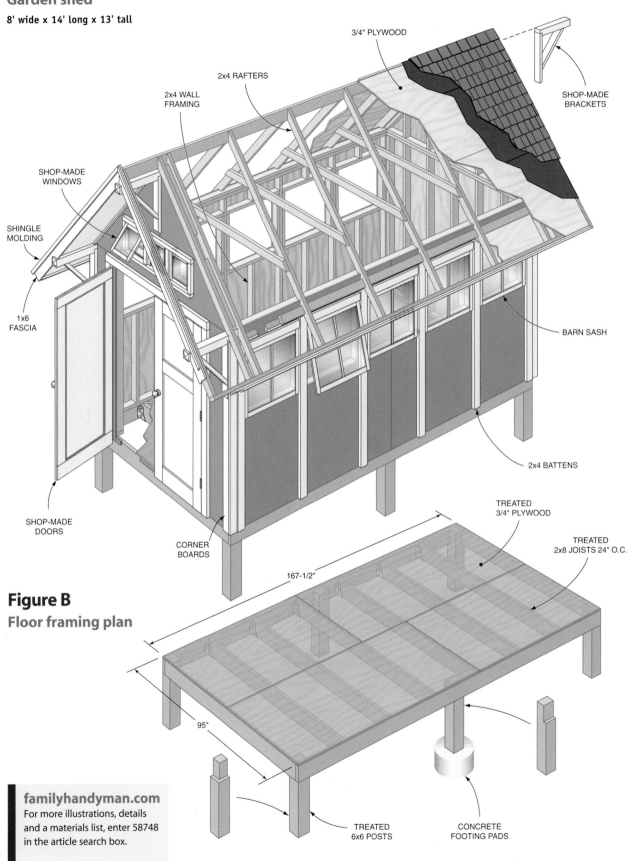

Figure A
Garden shed
8' wide x 14' long x 13' tall

3/4" PLYWOOD

2x4 RAFTERS

2x4 WALL FRAMING

SHOP-MADE BRACKETS

SHOP-MADE WINDOWS

SHINGLE MOLDING

BARN SASH

1x6 FASCIA

2x4 BATTENS

SHOP-MADE DOORS

CORNER BOARDS

TREATED 3/4" PLYWOOD

TREATED 2x8 JOISTS 24" O.C.

167-1/2"

Figure B
Floor framing plan

95"

TREATED 6x6 POSTS

CONCRETE FOOTING PADS

familyhandyman.com
For more illustrations, details and a materials list, enter 58748 in the article search box.

Money, time and tools

The materials for this shed cost about $4,000. You'll find most of the materials in stock at home centers and lumberyards. However, a few items, like the rough-sawn cedar boards for the exterior trim and 5/8-in. rough-sawn plywood for the siding, may not be available in your area. If this is the case, ask the salesperson to suggest substitutes. The barn sash windows are available from some local window suppliers or online. You'll need a tool belt full of standard carpentry tools as well as a circular saw to build the shed. You'll also need a table saw and a power miter saw to cut parts for the triple-wide front window and double front doors. With a helper or two, you could have the platform and shell built in two or three days. Then expect to spend four or five more days completing the siding, trim, doors, windows and roofing.

Getting started

Several weeks before you start, check with your local building department to see whether a permit is required and to find out how close to the lot lines you can build. Then call 811 for instructions on how to locate buried utility lines.

The first step is to build the jig for locating the footings and posts. Start by screwing four 2x4s together to form a rectangle with interior dimensions of 95 in. x 167-1/2 in. You'll use this frame to position the footing holes and posts. Square the 2x4 frame by making sure the diagonal measurements from opposite corners are equal. Then screw a diagonal brace to the frame to hold it square.

Position the frame in your desired shed location and use it to mark the location of the six posts. Move the post hole centers 2-3/4 in. inside the frame. Dig the holes to the depth and diameter required in your area and pour 8-in.-deep concrete footing pads in the bottom of each hole. Let the concrete harden overnight. The next day, cut the posts to length and notch them to support the joists as shown in Figure B. Use a builder's level, laser level or level mason's line to mark the posts for cutting. Position the posts by toe-screwing them to the 2x4 layout frame. Be sure they're plumb. Then pack soil around the posts. Build the platform on the posts according to Figure B.

Build the walls

Snap chalk lines on the plywood deck, 3-1/2 in. from the edges of the platform, to indicate the inside edge of the walls. Cut the wall parts using the Web site details as a guide. Then build the first wall and align the bottom 2x4 with the chalk line so it's straight. Hold the wall in place temporarily with toe screws through the bottom plate (Photo

1 Use the shed floor as a wall-framing platform. Straighten the bottom plate and screw it to the floor. Adjust the top plate until the diagonal measurements are equal. Add screws to the top plate to hold the wall square.

2 Cover the walls faster and easier by nailing on siding before you raise the walls.

3 Screw braces to the tops of the walls before you raise them. Screw the lower end of the brace to the platform to support the wall temporarily.

1 inset). Measure diagonally to square the wall (Photo 1) and tack the top corners in place with toe screws.

With the bottom plate secured along the chalk line and the wall held square, it's safe to nail on the plywood siding (Photo 2). Make sure the plywood extends 1-7/8 in. past the bottom plate. The joint between the two center sheets of siding won't be covered by a 2x4 batten, so for the best appearance, keep the nails evenly spaced and drive them carefully to avoid dents. Complete the siding, then remove the toe screws and stand the wall (Photo 3).

Line up the bottom plate with the chalk line and drive 16d nails between each stud into the rim joist. Then temporarily brace the wall with 2x4s while you build and stand the opposite wall. Build the end walls, but don't install the plywood yet. Stand the end walls and nail them to the platform. Then nail the corners together with 16d nails and add the second top plate. Finally, use a 4-ft. level to plumb the front and back walls while you screw on diagonal braces to hold them square.

Finish the end walls by nailing on the siding. On the front wall, make sure to line up the top edge of the siding with the underside of the top wall plate to allow for the installation of the drip cap over the door (Figure D, familyhandyman.com). You'll fill in the upper part of the end walls after building the roof frame.

Frame the roof

Start by cutting the ridge to length and marking the rafter locations on it. Also mark the rafter locations on the top plates of the walls. Set the ridge board on temporary posts (Photo 5). Then cut out a pair of rafters, using Figure E (online) and Photo 4 as guides. Test the fit by holding the rafters in place against the ridge. If the ridge and bird's-mouth cuts fit tight, label one of the rafters as a pattern and use it to mark the remaining 2x4s for cutting. You'll need 16 rafters that match the pattern and four front and back rafters with shallower bird's-mouth cuts to accommodate the brackets. Nail pairs of rafters to the ridge with 16d nails (Photo 5). Line up the rafters with the marks on the top plates and secure them with metal framing anchors. Wait until after you've nailed the 2x4 subfascia to the rafter tails to install the rafters that make up the front and back overhangs. Complete the roof framing by nailing blocking between the rafters to support the soffit plywood.

Fill in the gable ends

Using Figure C (online) as a guide, cut 2x4s to fill in the area above the front and back walls. Start by cutting the sloped top plates and nailing them to the blocking between the rafters. Then lay out

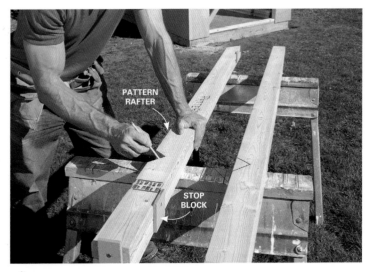

4 Cut one rafter and use it as a pattern to mark the others. Plywood stop blocks hold the pattern in position while you mark.

5 Position the ridge on temporary posts. Installing rafters is a lot easier if you have a helper at the other end.

6 Add the subfascia before you install the outermost rafters. The subfascia supports the outermost rafters and allows you to drive shims behind it to create a perfectly straight nailing surface for the fascia board.

the stud location on the top plate of the lower wall and use a level to transfer the marks to the sloped top plate. Measure between the marks to find the length of the studs. Frame the window openings on the front wall using the measurements in Figure C (online). Leave the siding off until after the doors are installed to allow for the drip cap installation.

The next step is to install the roof plywood (Photo 7). But before you do, check the top section of the end walls with a level to make sure they're plumb. If the walls aren't plumb, the roof will be out of square.

Build the doors and front window

Assemble the front doors using good-quality, straight 1x6 and 1x8 boards with plywood paneling inserts (Figure H, online). We've simplified the door-hanging process by mounting each door to a 2x4 and then screwing them separately to the wall. An easy way to mark and cut matching hinge recesses in both the door and the 2x4 is to clamp the 2x4 alongside the door, making sure the 2x4 extends 1/8 in. above the top of the door. Then mark the hinge cutout on both the door and the 2x4 at the same time. If you have a router, use a hinge-mortising bit to cut the hinge recesses. Otherwise use a sharp chisel. Screw the hinges to the door and 2x4 (Photo 8).

To hang the doors, line up a temporary 2x4 with the bottom of the siding and screw it to the wall. Then rest the doors on the 2x4 and use shims to create an even 1/8-in. space between them. Finally, drive 3-in. screws through the 2x4s into the framing to hold the doors in place (Photo 9). Finish the door installation by adding the top 2x4 trim piece and covering it with a metal drip cap (Figure G, online). Once the top door trim and drip cap are in place, cut and install the plywood siding that extends above the door. Stop these siding pieces 2-1/2 in. above the window opening to allow for the window drip cap.

Figure H (online) shows how to assemble the front window. Mount the window by screwing the window assembly on top of the plywood. Then install the drip cap and plywood above the window.

Install the exterior trim

Figure A shows the exterior trim details. The tricky part is installing pieces in the correct order. Start by mounting the brackets. Fit the two lower brackets into the notched rafters and screw them to the wall. Center the top bracket on the peak and push it tight to the rafters. Next, nail soffit plywood on the sides and front. Extend the side plywood to the outermost rafters. Wrap the corners with the corner boards, making sure to overlap the side boards

7 Nail blocks to the subfascia to support the plywood roof sheathing while you nail it on.

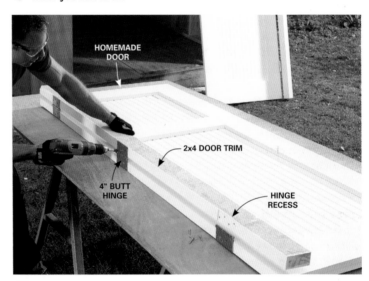

8 Hinge the doors to the side casings first. That way you can align the two doors easily and attach them by screwing the side casing to the shed.

9 Position the doors with a temporary ledger and shims. Then screw the side casings to the shed for a perfect fit.

onto the front boards so the batten spacing works out right (Figure G, online).

Next, nail a side batten alongside each side corner board. Wait to install the remaining battens. To simplify measuring, cut the 50-degree angle on the top of the corner and batten boards but leave them a little long. Push the angled end tight to the soffit and mark the lower end at the bottom of the siding. Get ready for roofing by adding the fascia boards and shingle molding. Photo 12 shows how the fascia boards are notched around the brackets. Keep the 1x2 shingle molding flush to the top of the roof plywood.

Rip 2x4s at a 50-degree angle and nail the beveled piece to the rafters to cover the seam between the soffit and the siding and to create a flat spot for the battens to butt against. Cut the battens to length and nail them to the studs between each window opening, taking care to position them parallel and an equal distance apart.

Hang the barn sash

The barn sash windows fit between the battens and on top of the siding. Just as with the front door mounting system, you start by mounting the sash to a board that's cut to fit between the battens (Photo 10). To prevent the windows from binding, make sure the edge of the board and the edge of the window are the same distance from the hinge (Photo 10, inset). Also make sure to center the window on the board. To help line up the window in the opening when you mount it, make a mark 1/2 in. from the bottom of the sash on the side that will face in. Line up the mark with the bottom of the window opening when you screw the board and window into place.

Photo 11 shows how to install the windows. You need a helper to screw the board and window from the inside because there's not enough space for a cordless drill under the soffit. Complete the window installation by screwing lid support hardware to the sides of the windows, about 8 in. from the bottom, and adding hook-and-eye locks and pulls.

Roof, stain and paint the shed

Complete the shed by installing shingles and finishing the exterior. For information on how to install shingles, go to familyhandyman.com and type "roofing" into the search box.

We stained and sealed the siding with a clear exterior stain finish. Prime and paint the trim, battens, doors and windows before installing them, then you only need to caulk and fill nail holes before rolling an additional coat of paint onto the flat surfaces.

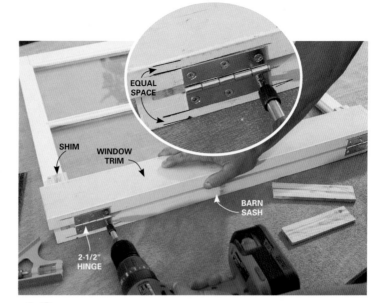

EQUAL SPACE

SHIM

WINDOW TRIM

BARN SASH

2-1/2" HINGE

10 Hang the windows using the same foolproof system you used for the doors. Cut lengths of trim to fit between the battens and attach the window to them with small butt hinges.

WINDOW TRIM

INSIDE HELPER

BARN SASH

11 Align the barn sash between the battens while a helper screws through the siding into the top trim piece from the inside.

NOTCH FASCIA

NOTCH FASCIA

12 Paint the exterior trim before you put it up. It'll save you a lot of time and allow you to protect even the back sides with primer and paint.

Weatherproof plant labels

Labeling rows of plants in a garden can be difficult.

Reader photo

Even permanent markers can't stand up to constant sun and moisture. Here's one solution: a label maker and recycled vinyl window blinds. Cut the slats into 9-in. lengths and stick on the labels. They stand up to any kind of weather without smearing, dissolving or rotting away.

Here's another easy way to keep a paper seed packet from getting destroyed by wind and rain out in your garden: Slip a small zipper-type plastic bag over the packet, with the bag upside down so the rain doesn't get in.

Backwoods repair kit

If you spend a lot of time outdoors, it's a good idea to carry a repair kit wherever you go.

Of course, the kit varies depending on the trip, but here are a few standard items. Some are pretty obvious, like duct tape, paracord, zip ties and a multi-tool.

But the others aren't: A piece of aluminum tube that can slide over a broken tent pole can be a trip saver. A lightweight magnifier will actually allow you to see what you're doing when you make small repairs.

And thin wire is one of the most useful items you can carry. Wrap it, twist it, "sew" with it .... It's strong, heat-proof and doesn't stretch. You can use it to fix everything from a boot to a canoe.

MAGNIFIER

THIN WIRE

ALUMINUM TUBE

Easy access, storage galore and
a private porch add up to

Shed plus shelter

This shed has a large sliding door on one end to access the 8 x 16-ft. storage area, three windows for lots of light and a front entry door for extra convenience. But the best feature is the large covered porch where you can work on projects or just hang out in the shade with friends. The front half of the roof is supported by 6x6 posts and 2x10 beams. We continued the post-and-beam look on the rest of the shed, using the 2x10 beams to support the wide roof overhangs. We used inexpensive standard framing lumber for the beams and corner boards, and coated it with a super-durable finish to give it a rich, rustic appearance. The windows are aluminum storm windows. The front door is a steel entry door purchased at a home center.

Cost, time and tools

You can find most of the materials for this shed at your local home center or lumberyard. But you'll have to special-order the windows and the sliding door hardware. See the Materials List at familyhandyman.com/2012shed for ordering information.

WHAT IT TAKES **Time:** 4–5 weekends
Skill level: Advanced

In this article, we'll show you the important steps of how to build the shed. For more details on wall and roof framing and information on how to build the sliding doors, go to familyhandyman.com/2012shed

1 Stand and brace the walls. Build the walls flat on the slab and then stand them up. Plumb the corners with a level and nail diagonal braces to the walls. Straighten the top plate by stretching a string over spacer blocks at each end. Gauge the straightness with a third block. When the top plate is straight, nail the brace.

As with any larger construction project, you'll need a set of standard carpentry tools plus a circular saw and drill. We used a framing nail gun to speed up the wall and roof framing and a miter saw for the exterior trim work, but hammers and a circular saw will do the job. You'll have to rip boards for the windowsill and some of the other trim parts. A table saw works best for this.

Before you start building

At least a month before you plan to build, check with your local building department to see if a permit is required. You may have to supply a survey to show where the shed is located on the property. We hired a concrete contractor to pour the slab, but if you decide to tackle this part of the project yourself, you can find instructions on our Web site. Go to familyhandyman.com and search for "concrete slab." A few days before you plan to dig, call 811 for instructions on how to locate buried utility lines.

You'll save time and get a better job if you prefinish the beams, trim and grooved plywood for the overhang ceiling. Then all you have to do is touch up the cut ends after the parts are installed. We used a log and siding finish for the posts, beams and corner trim (search for "log and siding finish" online). It's expensive but looks great and is very durable. Then we put two coats of clear exterior finish on the cedar plywood siding and the grooved roof plywood (Photo 8).

2 Mark the post notches. Temporarily position and brace the posts. Then use one of the beams as a giant straightedge to mark the post notches. Align the beam with the top plate of the side wall, tack it into place and mark the post. Do the same thing on the other end. Then snap a chalk line between the two marks to mark the inner posts.

3 Cut the notches. Mark 1-1/2-in.-deep notches on both sides of the posts. Cut as much as you can with a circular saw. Complete the notches with a handsaw.

Build the walls

Start by measuring 3-1/2 in. from the outside edge of the slab on the back and sides and snapping chalk lines to mark the interior edge of the bottom plate. Then measure from the back line to mark the location of the front bottom plate and snap a line. Now measure between the pairs of opposite lines to make sure they're parallel, and measure diagonally

Figure A Shed

Overall Dimensions: 16' x 16'

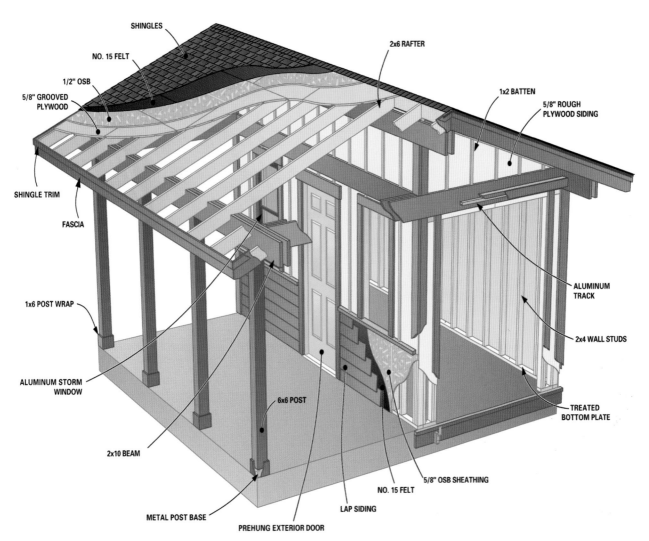

- SHINGLES
- NO. 15 FELT
- 1/2" OSB
- 5/8" GROOVED PLYWOOD
- SHINGLE TRIM
- FASCIA
- 1x6 POST WRAP
- ALUMINUM STORM WINDOW
- METAL POST BASE
- 2x10 BEAM
- 6x6 POST
- PREHUNG EXTERIOR DOOR
- LAP SIDING
- NO. 15 FELT
- 5/8" OSB SHEATHING
- 2x6 RAFTER
- 1x2 BATTEN
- 5/8" ROUGH PLYWOOD SIDING
- ALUMINUM TRACK
- 2x4 WALL STUDS
- TREATED BOTTOM PLATE

Figure B

Shed door

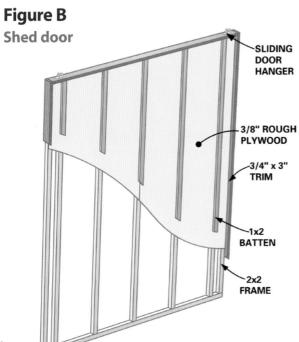

- SLIDING DOOR HANGER
- 3/8" ROUGH PLYWOOD
- 3/4" x 3" TRIM
- 1x2 BATTEN
- 2x2 FRAME

from corner to corner (where the chalk lines intersect). The diagonal measurements should be equal. If not, the slab is not square and you should cheat the lines as needed until the diagonal measurements are equal. If you skip this step, you risk fighting with an out-of-square building for the entire project. With chalk lines snapped, you can cut the 2x4 plates to length and mark the stud and window and door openings on them according to the plans. Go to familyhandyman.com/ 2012shed for more details.

Drill holes in the treated bottom plates for the anchor bolts. Then build the walls. Lay the plates for the back wall on the slab and spread the studs between them, aligning them with the marks. Nail the plates to the studs. Stand the back wall—you'll have to lift it over the anchor bolts—and support it with temporary braces on each end. Align the bottom plate with the chalk line and tighten the anchor bolts.

Build, stand and temporarily brace the front wall. Then build the side walls. When all of the walls are up, nail the corners together and nail the second top plates to the back and side walls, overlapping the plates at the corners. Finally, check

4 Set the beams. Stand the posts and brace them. Mark the post locations on the first beam. Align the posts with the marks and connect them with screws. Screw the second beam to the other side of the posts.

5 Install the rafters. Cut the ridge to length and mark the rafter locations on it. Also mark the rafter locations on the front beam and the top plate of the back wall.

the corners with a level to make sure they're plumb, and nail diagonal braces across the studs on the inside to hold them in place. Also straighten the top plates using a taut string and braces (Photo 1).

Nail the plywood siding to the back wall. We used 5/8-in.-thick rough-sawn plywood without any grooves, but you could substitute any good-looking exterior plywood. To cut costs, we substituted 5/8-in. oriented strand board in the area under the windows that would be covered by siding.

Stand the front posts and beams

The front half of the roof is supported by four 6x6 cedar posts that are notched to accept both 2x10 beams. Photo 2 shows how we set them up for marking the location of the notches. Rest the bottom of the posts on the metal post brackets and temporarily brace them. We used screws for all the temporary bracing because they're easy to put in and take out. Use one of the 2x10 beams to mark the end post as shown in the photo. Do the same thing on the opposite end, and then snap a chalk line between the marks to mark the center for notching.

Number the posts so you get them back in the right spot. Then take them down and cut the notches (Photo 3). Finish up by putting the posts back in place. Use a level to plumb the posts and brace them with pairs of 2x4s. Then cut the front 2x10 beams to length and mark the post locations on them. Line the posts up with the marks and screw the posts and beams together (Photo 4).

Frame the roof

Cut the 2x6 rafters according to the dimensions online at

6 Fill in the gable-end studs. Cut angles on the top plate and screw it to the underside of the rafter. Make marks every 16 in. Measure and cut the studs and nail them in.

familyhandyman.com/2012shed. Mark the 2x6 ridge, the top plate of the back wall and the top of the front beam with the rafter locations. The rafters are 2-ft. on center. Nail or screw the ridge to the top of the front wall. Check the plans online for the exact position of the ridge. Also cut and attach the 2x10 beam that runs along the top of the back wall, making sure it protrudes 2 ft. on each end. Now you're ready to install the rafters (Photo 5). We used 3-in. screws to attach the rafters, but 16d framing nails will also work.

7 Add the false beams. Screw 2-1/2-in. spacer blocks to the protruding beam ends. Then screw or nail on the false beam.

8 Sheathe the roof—twice! Sheathe the roof with a layer of decorative grooved plywood so the underside of the roof looks good from below. Then add another layer of OSB so the roofing nails don't pop through.

Complete the wall frame and siding

With the roof frame in place, you can fill in the short studs on each end wall. Start by cutting angles on the ends of the top plate and screwing or nailing it to the underside of the rafter. Then mark the location of the studs (Photo 6). Measure and cut the studs and nail them in.

Finish the walls by nailing the cedar plywood siding to the top of the front and side walls. You can cut the window and door openings before or after installing the plywood siding.

Complete the beams

The remaining beams are decorative. One snugs to the underside of the rafters on the front wall. Two more run between the front and the back beams. After these are in place, add the 2-1/2-in. spacers (Photo 7) and the decorative second half of all the beams. Finally cut a 2x10 to fit horizontally between the side beams, above the door and windows, and nail it to the front wall.

Sheathe the roof

For a more finished looking ceiling, we installed 4 x 8-ft. sheets of 8-in. on-center grooved pine siding, face side down, over the rafters (Photo 8). Then we covered this with a layer of 1/2-in. OSB so the roofing nails wouldn't poke through.

Build the sliding door

Screw 2x2s together to form the frame for the sliding door according to the details online. Then nail 3/8-in.-thick cedar plywood to the 2x2s and wrap the perimeter with 1x4s ripped to 3 in. Nail the 1x4s flush with the back of the 2x2s so they

9 Hang the door track. Attach a track support to the beam with 1/4 x 5-in. lag screws to support the track. Then screw the aluminum track to the support.

protrude past the siding. The 1x4s will cover the ends of the battens.

We used heavy-duty bypass door hardware to support the exterior sliding door. The parts are easy to order online (see the Materials List online), and the three-wheel hangers operate smoothly. Attach the 2x4 track support to the 2x10 beam with 1/4-in. x 5-in. lag screws. Then screw the tracks to the underside of the 2x4, spacing them about 1/4 in. from the beam (Photo 9).

FRONT OF DOOR

HANGER BRACKET

THREE-WHEEL HANGER

NOTCH

MITER

10 Mount the hangers. Screw the hanger brackets to the top of the sliding door. Slide the three-wheel hangers into the track. Lift the door to the track and connect the hangers to the hanger brackets.

11 Wrap the front and side with a sill. Cut 10-degree bevels on 2x4s to form the angled sill. Notch the sills to fit into the window opening. Then mark for the miters where they intersect at the outside corner. Cut the miters and nail the sill to the wall, making sure it runs level.

Mount the hanger brackets to the top of the door as shown in Photo 10. Slide the wheel assemblies into the track and screw a block of wood into the open end of the track to prevent the door from rolling off the end. Then hang the door on the track by clipping the wheel assemblies into the hanger brackets.

Close the gap between the bottom of the door and the concrete slab by attaching a sill with polyurethane construction adhesive and concrete screws (see plans online). Then, to prevent the door from swinging out, screw a bent steel "bar holder" (search online for "zinc open bar holder") onto a spacer block that allows enough clearance for the door to slide. Finish the installation by covering the track and mounting board with a 1x4 trim board.

Install the entry door and windows

We bought a standard 3-ft.-wide steel entry door from a home center, removed the molding and installed it in the front wall. For more information on how to install a door, go to family-handyman.com and search for "door install." Install the front door and windowsill before mounting the windows. Nail 1-in. x 4-in. trim boards to the sides of the front door and use a 2x6 for the top trim. We cut the window and door trim from 1-in.-thick cedar decking.

Make the angled sill piece by ripping a 10-degree bevel on the front and back edge of a 2x4. Notch the sill pieces to protrude 1 in. into the window openings. Then mark where they intersect at the outside corner and cut the miters (Photo 11). Be sure to tilt the sill at a 10-degree angle in your miter saw

1x3 SHINGLE MOLDING

1x8 FASCIA

12 Trim the roof. Install the 1x8 fascia boards and the 1x3 shingle molding. Make sure the 1x3 shingle molding is lined up with the roof surface.

when you're cutting the miters. Do this by pressing the beveled side tight to the fence.

The custom-size aluminum storm windows we used have 1-in.-thick expandable U-shaped channels around the perimeter for mounting. We nailed 1x2s to the sides and top of the framed openings, 1 in. back from the face of the siding and screwed the windows to these (Photo 14). If you use storm windows with thin mounting flanges, relocate these nailing strips to 1/8 in. behind the face of the siding. See the Materials List online for window-ordering details.

STAGGERED ENDS

13 Nail on the shingles. Staple roofing felt over the sheathing, overlapping the seams about 3 in. Then nail on the shingles according to the manufacturer's instructions. Cover the ridge with ridge shingles.

Finish the exterior

The corners are covered with 2x6 SPF lumber to look like posts. The front corners are a little tricky because the 2x6s have to be cut to fit onto the angled sill. The easiest solution is to rip the 2x6s to form a 45-degree bevel on one long edge. Then cut the 10-degree angle on the bottom (where they sit on the sill) and join the bevels to form the corner.

You can start roofing anytime after you've finished installing the fascia trim (Photo 12). It's a good idea to cover the roof with roofing paper as soon as possible to keep everything dry. Then shingle the roof (Photo 13) and cover the ridge with ridge shingles. For information on how to install shingles, go to familyhandyman.com and search for "roofing."

We installed 1/2-in. x 7-1/4-in. rough-cedar lap siding (Photo 15) under the windows and finished the cedar plywood siding with 1x2 battens nailed to the studs every 16 in. Cover the OSB with No. 15 building paper before you install the siding. If you use the same size siding, you'll have six courses with 5-1/2 in. of the siding exposed on each course. Start by ripping the top piece of siding to 5-1/2 in. and using the leftover strip as a starter under the first course. Align it with the bottom edge of the bottom plate and nail it on. Then nail the first course of siding over this. Continue with the remaining pieces, overlapping them to leave 5-1/2 in. of the previous course exposed.

Touch up the paint and stain and install the door hardware and you're ready to pull up some chairs to enjoy your new hangout.

ALUMINUM STORM WINDOW

1x2 STOP

SILL

14 Install the windows. Nail 1x2 stops to the top and sides of the openings. Set the window in the opening and slide the expandable U-shaped channels tight to the framing. Screw through the channels into the stops to secure the windows.

5-1/2"

LAP SIDING

15 Install siding below the windows. Make chalk lines to indicate the top edge of each row of siding. Line the siding up with the lines and nail it to the studs. Leave a 1/16-in. gap at each end and fill them with caulk later.

Pine garden hutch

Wouldn't it be nice to have all your gardening tools and supplies in one handy location? This copper-roofed pine hutch holds long-handled tools like shovels, rakes and hoes on one side, and smaller tools and supplies on shelves on the other side.

Start by building the face frame

Build the face frame (Photo 3) first and use it as a guide for assembling the doors and cutting the curve on the back panel.

A full sheet of 3/4-in. MDF (medium-density fiberboard) or particleboard set on sawhorses makes a good workbench for this project. Set up for marking the arcs (for the curved pieces) by drawing a center line parallel to the long edge of the sheet. Center a 4-ft. length of 1x12 on the line. Line up the top edge with the edge of the workbench and clamp it. Screw the point of the homemade compass in the center line 21-5/8 in. below the bottom edge of the 1x12 (Photo 1). Draw three arcs for the face frame top and door top pieces (Figure B, p. 100). Then replace the 1x12 with another 48-in. 1x12 and relocate the screw point (see Figure B). Draw two arcs to outline the 1-1/2-in.-wide curved roof trim molding. Cut out the curves (Photo 2).

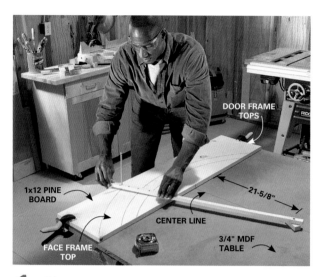

1 Build a large compass by drilling holes in a 36-in.-long stick using Figure B as a guide. Draw arcs for the face frame top (A1) and door frame tops (D) on a 4-ft. 1x12. On a second 4-ft. 1x12, draw arcs for the curved molding (A2) under the front roof (Figure B, p. 100).

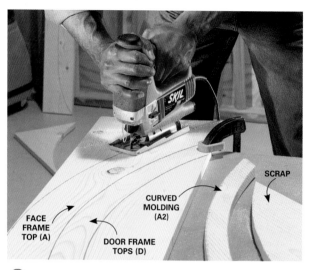

2 Saw out the curved pieces with a jigsaw. Use the pattern on p. 100 to draw the curve on the face frame bottom (C1) and saw it out.

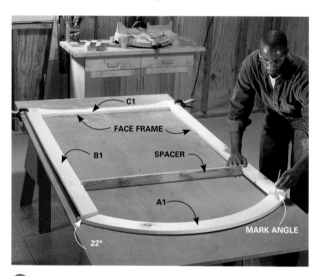

3 Cut the side pieces (B1) to length with 22-degree angles on the tops. Snug the face frame sides to the bottom (C1) and to a 39-in.-long spacer and clamp them to the table. Scribe lines on the curved top (A1) and cut off the ends.

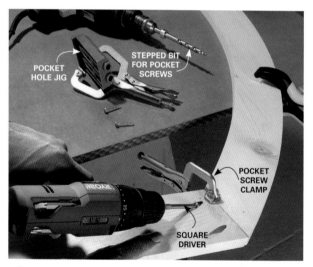

4 Drill pocket holes on the back side of the face frame pieces with a pocket hole jig. Glue the joints and connect them with pocket screws.

Even with careful jigsaw work, you'll need to sand the curves smooth. Use 80-grit sandpaper on a sanding block to even out the curve and remove saw marks. Then sand again with 100- and 120-grit paper. For the best-looking finish, sand all the boards before assembly. Use a random orbital sander or hand-sand with the grain of the wood.

After cutting and sanding the curved pieces, rip the remaining face frame and door trim pieces to width and cut them to length according to Figure A and the Cutting List, both on p. 100. Use the pattern on p. 100 to cut the curve on the 39-in.-long 1x6 bottom frame piece (C1). Cut the same curve on the 44-in.-long x 5-in.-wide piece (C2). Use this for the bottom cleat (Photo 5). Assemble the face frames and door frames and the back frame with pocket screws. Photos 3 and 6 show how to mark

for the angle cuts where the curved pieces join the straight ones.

Use a miter box to cut angles on the ends of the curved pieces, and steady them by supporting them with one of the scrap concave corners cut from the 1x12. Place the straight edge of the concave scrap against the fence and nestle the curves. Then sight along the blade and adjust the angle to cut along the line. Use this same technique for cutting the angles on the ends of the curved door frame tops (D) as shown in Photo 6.

After assembling the face frame, flip it over and screw on the cleats (B2 and C2; Photo 5). The cleats overlap the joints to add strength and serve as a nailing surface for the floorboards and side panels.

Cutting list

KEY	PCS.	SIZE & DESCRIPTION
Face frame		
A1, D	1	48" x 3/4" x 11-1/4" (curved frame and door tops)
A2	1	48" x 3/4" x 11-1/4" (curved molding; cut curve and ends)
B1	2	68" x 3/4" x 3-1/2" (sides)*
B2	2	66" x 3/4" x 2-1/2" (side cleats)*
C1	1	39" x 3/4" x 5-1/2" (bottom; cut curve to pattern)
C2	1	44" x 3/4" x 5" (bottom cleat; cut curve to pattern)
Doors		
D	2	Curved tops (cut from "door top" above)
E1	2	68-5/8" x 3/4" x 2-1/4" (door sides)*
E2	2	61" x 3/4" x 2-1/4" (door sides)*
F1	2	14-13/16" x 3/4" x 2-1/4" (door bottom rail); see Figure B
F2	4	14-13/16" x 3/4" x 4" (intermediate rails)
G	6	72" t&g 1x8 (door panels); cut to fit
Sides		
H	6	68-1/4" t&g 1x8 (19-1/2" x 68-1/4" side panels)
J	2	5" x 3/4" x 17-1/4" (bottom cleats)
K	2	5-1/2" x 3/4" x 17-1/4" (top cleats; bevel top to 45 degrees)
Back		
L	7	78" t&g 1x8 (44" x 78" back panel; cut top curve)
M	2	3-1/2" x 3/4" x 68" (frame sides)
N	3	3-1/2" x 3/4" x 37" (frame crosspiece)
P	1	5" x 3/4" x 42-1/2" (bottom cleat)
Interior parts		
Q	1	2" x 3/4" x 16-1/2" (floor crosspiece)
R	2	9" x 3/4" x 44" (floorboards)
S	3	72" t&g 1x8 (17-1/4" x 72" center panel)
T1	1	3/4" x 3/4" x 72" (center panel cleats)
T2	2	3/4" x 3/4" x 17-1/4" (center panel cleats)
U	8	1-1/2" x 3/4" x 17-1/4" (shelf cleats)
V	8	8-5/8" x 3/4" x 21-5/8" (shelf boards)
W	3	3-1/2" x 3/4" x 21-1/2" (roof boards)
X	18	2-1/2" x 3/4" x 21-1/2" (roof boards)

*Cut top angles at 22 degrees.

Figure A Garden hutch

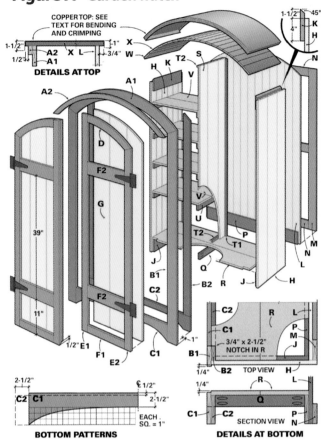

COPPER TOP: SEE TEXT FOR BENDING AND CRIMPING

DETAILS AT TOP

BOTTOM PATTERNS

EACH SQ. = 1"

TOP VIEW

DETAILS AT BOTTOM

SECTION VIEW

NOTCH IN R

Materials list

ITEM	QTY.
1x2 x 8' pine	3
1x3 x 8' pine	9
1x4 x 6' pine	4
1x4 x 8' pine	3
1x6 x 6' pine	4
1x10 x 8' pine	3
1x12 x 8' pine	1
1x8 x 6' t&g pine	15
1x8 x 8' t&g pine	7
8" gate hinges	4
Latch	1
Tubes of construction adhesive	2
Magnetic catches	4
Water-resistant wood glue	
1-1/4" finish nails	
Copper or brass weatherstrip nails	
Pocket screws and jig	
2' x 5' 16-oz. copper sheet (Available from roofing or sheet metal suppliers)	

Figure B Arc patterns

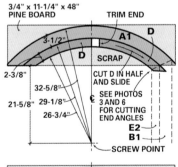

3/4" x 11-1/4" x 48" PINE BOARD

TRIM END

CUT D IN HALF AND SLIDE
SEE PHOTOS 3 AND 6 FOR CUTTING END ANGLES

SCREW POINT

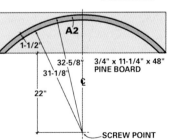

3/4" x 11-1/4" x 48" PINE BOARD

SCREW POINT

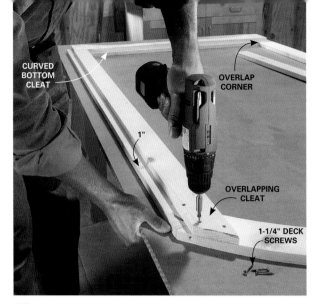

CURVED BOTTOM CLEAT

OVERLAP CORNER

1"

OVERLAPPING CLEAT

1-1/4" DECK SCREWS

5 Cut backing cleats (B2 and C2) that overlap the face frame joints (Figure A, parts A1, B1 and C1). Predrill and screw them to the back of the face frame.

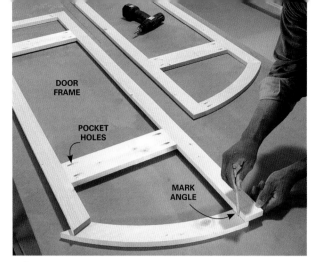

DOOR FRAME

POCKET HOLES

MARK ANGLE

6 Assemble the door frame with pocket screws as shown. Then cut the curved top (D) in half and cut angles on the ends to fit. Attach them with pocket screws as well. Place the assembled door frames in the face frame to check the fit. Plane and sand as needed to allow a 1/8-in. space around and between the door frames.

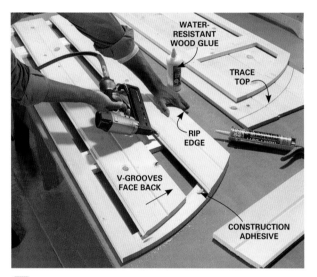

WATER-RESISTANT WOOD GLUE

TRACE TOP

RIP EDGE

V-GROOVES FACE BACK

CONSTRUCTION ADHESIVE

7 Temporarily assemble the door panels and center the frames over them. Mark the bottom, sides and top. Rip the sides and cut the top curve. Cut the bottoms 1/4 in. shorter than marked. Then glue and nail the boards together with wood glue and fasten them to the frame with construction adhesive.

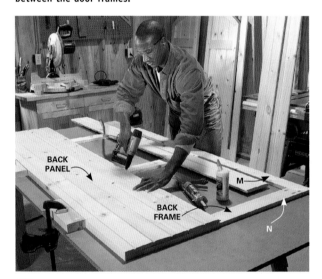

BACK PANEL

M

BACK FRAME

N

8 Assemble the back frame (M and N) with pocket screws. Glue and nail tongue-and-groove boards to it to form the cabinet back. Rip the first and last boards to fit.

Take time building the doors

Use the completed face frame as a guide to check the fit of the doors as they're built. The goal is to end up with a 1/8-in. space between the doors and the face frame and between the two doors. Sand or plane them as needed to create an even gap. Build and fit the door frames first. Then use them as a guide to cut out the tongue-and-groove boards that make up the door panels (Photo 7). Rip the groove off the first board in each door panel and then rip the last board to fit. Glue and nail the boards to the frames and then sand the edges flush. A belt sander works great for this task.

Build the side and back panels

The panels for the sides and back are constructed just like the door panels. Rip the tongues and grooves from the outermost boards after figuring out how wide they should be (Photo 8).

The exact ripping widths will probably vary between projects, based on the boards that are used. The easiest approach is to temporarily assemble the tongue-and-groove boards, using clamps if needed to draw them tight together. Then mark the panel widths on them, making sure to measure over the panel to remove an equal amount from the outside boards. Rip the outside boards to width. Then assemble the panels. Run a small bead of water-resistant wood glue along the tongue of each board before sliding it into the groove. Clean up any squeezed-out glue right away with a damp cloth. When the glue hardens, the panels will be rigid and strengthen the cabinet. Use construction adhesive to glue the panels to the frames and/or cleats.

Here are a few special considerations for building the panels. First, use a framing square to make sure the panels are perfectly square before the glue dries. Cut the curve on the back

9 Center the face frame over the back panel and line up the bottoms. Mark the top curve. Saw it out with a jigsaw.

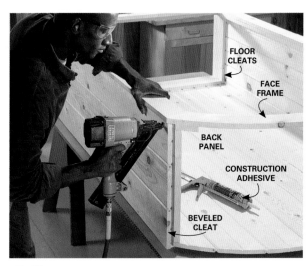

10 Assemble the side panels (Figure A). Then glue and nail the side panels to the back panel and the face frame.

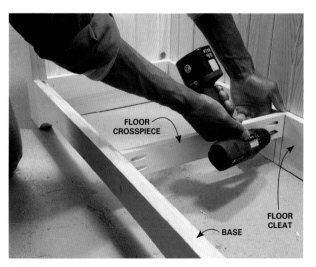

11 Screw in the crosspiece (Q) with pocket screws to support the floorboards. Notch the first floorboard (R) to fit around the face frame and glue and nail it down. Cut the back floorboard to fit and nail it in.

12 Glue and nail together the center divider and attach it to the bottom and back with cleats (T1 and T2) and screws. Attach the top to the ceiling boards after they're installed (Photo 13).

panel after it's constructed (Photo 9). The beveled top cleat (K) on the side panels (H) is a little tricky. Study Photos 10 and 13 and Figure A to see its location and orientation.

Assemble the cabinet, then mount the doors

Glue and nail the completed panels and face frame together (Photo 10). Then add the floorboards and center panel (Photo 12). Center the curved molding (A2) and nail it to the top of the face frame. Finally, glue and nail the roof boards along the curve (Photo 13). Start with 1x4s aligned with the ends of the curved molding. Then complete the roof with 1x3s, working from both sides to the center. To make sure everything is square, temporarily tack the 1x4 in place. Then set four of the 1x3s on the roof with their ends perfectly aligned and measure

the front overhang to make sure it's consistent. If the overhang is getting larger or smaller, move the back end of the 1x4 down or up, respectively, to correct the problem.

When the cabinet is complete, tip it on its back to install the doors (Photo 14). Use any strong gate-type hinge. Just make sure to leave an even space around the perimeter of the doors and between them. Use a belt sander to trim tight spots.

Crimping tool simplifies curve of the metal roof

Start with a 24-in. x 60-in. piece of 16-oz. copper sheeting. Screw down a 2x4 frame on the bench top to provide clearance for bending down the edges. Start by snipping the corners of the copper with tin snips (Photo 15). Then hand-bend the edges of the sheet down over the 2x4s. The last step is to crimp

13 Nail the curved molding (A2) to the face frame. Then glue and nail the ceiling boards to the top of the cabinet. Start by overhanging the 1x4s as shown and work from both sides to the center with the 1x3 boards. Cut the last piece to fit.

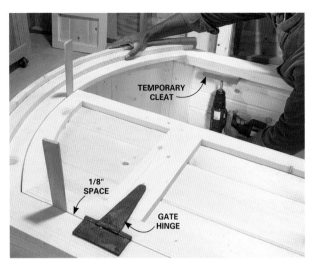

14 Screw temporary cleats to the back of the face frame to support the doors. Set the doors in place and trim them if necessary to allow 1/8-in. clearance all around. Predrill for hinge screws and screw on the door hinges and hardware.

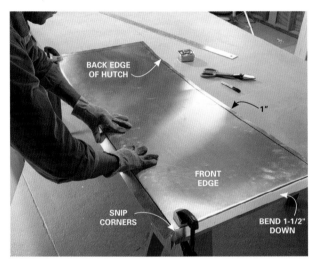

15 Center the 24-in.-wide copper sheet over the cabinet top with a 1-1/2-in. overhang in front. Mark along the back, front and ends with a permanent marker. Add 1-1/2 in. to the ends and cut the copper sheet to length with tin snips. Snip the corners as shown. Bend the front, back and ends down over the 2x4 frame.

16 Crimp the front and back edges to form the curved top using a special sheet metal crimping tool. Alternate between the front and the back until you reach the end.

the edges with the five-blade downspout crimper to curve the sheet (Photo 16). Keep the crimps parallel by aligning one of the crimping blades in the previously made crimp before squeezing it. Crimp about 12 in. on the front. Then crimp 24 in. on the back to even up the curve. Continue alternating until the end. Adjust the arch for an exact fit once the copper is back on top of the cabinet. Hold off on nailing the copper in place (Photo 17) until after a finish has been applied to the hutch.

Since the hutch is pine and will rot quickly if left unprotected outdoors, apply a durable finish. This hutch has an oil stain and three coats of spar varnish. Be sure to seal the bottom edges thoroughly. If putting the hutch in a wet location, install metal or plastic feet on all four corners to elevate it slightly. Setting the hutch on an uneven surface can cause the doors to bind or fit poorly. Shim under the cabinet to level it, if needed.

17 Drill 1/16-in. pilot holes (through the copper only) about every 12 in. along the edges. Drive small copper or brass weather-strip nails through the copper into the wood slats to hold the copper roofing in place.

Window planter

You can build and finish several of these simple window planters in a day. For each planter, you'll need three 6-in. clay pots, 3 ft. each of 1x10 and 1x3, and 2 ft. of 2x8.

Cut the 1x10 and 1x3 to length (see photos for dimensions). Pot diameters vary, so size the holes by scribing and cutting out a 6-in. circle from cardboard to ensure that the pot will rest on its rim (Photo 1). Keep testing until you find the size. Then lay out and cut the openings.

Use a 5-gallon pail lid to scribe the bracket curves (Photo 2). Make sure the grain runs parallel to the shelf for strength. Smooth off the rough edges and paint the parts before assembly—especially if you want the two-tone look. Then screw the parts together with 2-in. exterior screws.

Mount the shelf to the wall by screwing through the hanging strip into the wall framing.

WHAT IT TAKES

Time: 2 hours
Skill level: Beginner

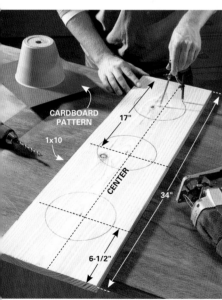

1 Mark the 6-in.-diameter holes with a compass. Then drill 1/2-in. starter holes and cut out the openings with a jigsaw.

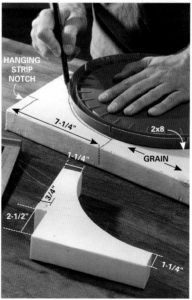

2 Mark the notch for the hanging strip and both 1-1/4-in. ends on the brackets. Draw the curve and cut the openings with a jigsaw.

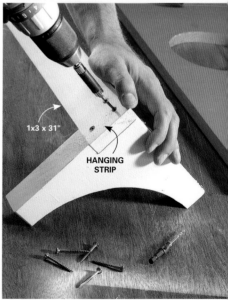

3 Predrill and screw the hanging strip to the brackets. Then center and screw the shelf to the brackets and to the hanging strip.

6
Tools & materials

Tool tray tower

BUILT-IN PULL

WHAT IT TAKES **Time:** 4 hours
Skill level: Intermediate

Because most hand tools are relatively flat, piling them in deep drawers wastes a lot of space and makes them hard to find and dig out. This rather fetching cabinet separates and organizes all those tools. Best of all, you can remove the tray containing, say, the open-end wrenches, and take the whole collection to wherever you're wrenching.

There are several plain versions of this design: a few drawers made from MDF with utilitarian handles. We decided to bump it up a notch and build a 10-tray unit out of cabinet-grade birch plywood. And rather than use handles, we made the tray bases with built-in "paddle pulls."

Shaping the paddle pulls is the trickiest part of the whole project. You'll get the best results by clamping the tray bottoms together and gang-cutting the paddle pulls all at once with a band saw. Sanding them all at once also saves lots of time and ensures that the parts are identical (Photo 5). (Then get the alternating paddle pulls by flipping over half of the tray bottoms.)

If you don't have a band saw, a jigsaw will do. If you're jigsawing, mark one paddle

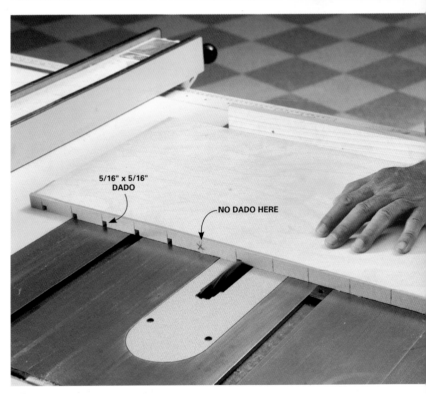

5/16" x 5/16" DADO

NO DADO HERE

1 Mark and cut the dadoes for the drawers. Mark the dado bottoms on the edges beginning at 13/16 in. up from the bottom and then every 2 in. Don't cut a dado in the center—that's where the stretcher goes. After cutting all 10 dadoes, cut off the top, 2-3/4 in. above the last dado bottom.

pull on a tray bottom and use it to scribe and gang-cut five at a time. You can also just skip the paddle pulls and add the drawer pulls of your choice. To do that, cut the tray bottoms to 15-1/2 x 12 in., but "gang-sand" them all as shown in Photo 5.

This project calls for a table saw and a dado blade. The good news is that absolutely no hardware is needed, including fussy, expensive drawer slides to mess around with.

This project is a real plywood eater. You'll need a full sheet of both 1/4-in. and 3/4-in. plywood to build one. Build it with more or fewer trays; it's up to you. If you choose to make a wider or taller cabinet with more trays, fine. But it'll take more than two sheets of plywood!

Cut the back and sides a little oversize

Cut the 1/4-in. back first. Take a notch out of a corner of the sheet rather than ripping a whole strip or you won't have enough left-over plywood to make the drawer bases. Cut the back 1/8 in. larger than the illustration calls for. After the cabinet is assembled, you can get extremely accurate measurements and either cut the back to fit or use a flush-trim router bit after it's attached. Cut the sides

2 Prefinish the interior surfaces. Protect the gluing areas with masking tape and varnish surfaces on the cabinet interior. It's much easier to do now than later. For smooth tray operation, be sure to brush out any varnish pools or drips inside the dadoes.

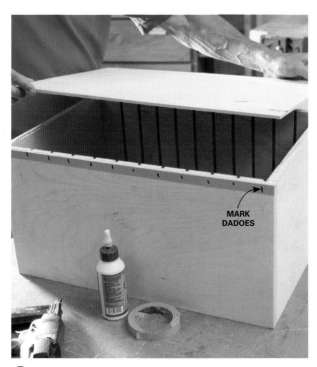

3 Assemble the box. Glue and nail the box together with 1-1/2-in. brads. Then mark the dadoes to avoid misses when you nail on the back with 1-in. brads. Glue the perimeter, then nail one edge flush with the box side. Square up the box with the back to nail the second side. Then finish nailing the remaining two sides.

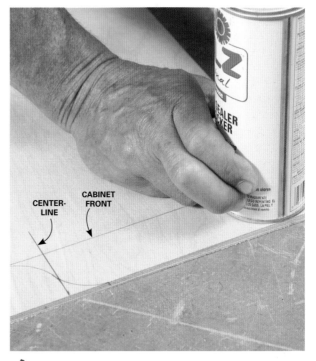

4 Mark the paddle pulls. Cut the tray bottoms into 15-1/2 x 13-3/4-in. rectangles. Draw a line 12 in. from the back edge of the trays and mark a centerline. Use the centerline and one of the corners as a guide while you trace around a spray paint can to mark the curves. Then cut the shapes with a band saw or jigsaw.

Figure A
Tool tray tower

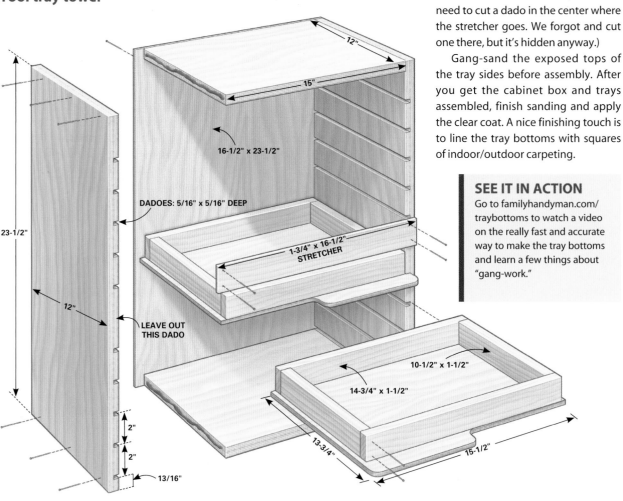

12"

15"

16-1/2" x 23-1/2"

DADOES: 5/16" x 5/16" DEEP

23-1/2"

1-3/4" x 16-1/2"
STRETCHER

12"

LEAVE OUT
THIS DADO

10-1/2" x 1-1/2"

14-3/4" x 1-1/2"

2"

2"

13/16"

13-3/4"

15-1/2"

a full 24 in. tall and cut them to length after the dadoes are cut. (You don't need to cut a dado in the center where the stretcher goes. We forgot and cut one there, but it's hidden anyway.)

Gang-sand the exposed tops of the tray sides before assembly. After you get the cabinet box and trays assembled, finish sanding and apply the clear coat. A nice finishing touch is to line the tray bottoms with squares of indoor/outdoor carpeting.

SEE IT IN ACTION
Go to familyhandyman.com/traybottoms to watch a video on the really fast and accurate way to make the tray bottoms and learn a few things about "gang-work."

5 Gang-sand the tray bottoms. Clamp the tray bottoms together and sand the fronts of them all at once. Get them roughed out and then finish up with a random orbital sander. (If you have a dedicated drum sander or drum sander accessory for your drill press, use that for the inside curves.)

OVERHANG MARK

CENTERING BLOCK

6 Build the trays. Glue and nail the tray sides together. Center one of the bottoms with equal overhangs, then mark a centering block to guide you while you glue and nail on the bottoms. You'll need to use the block on just one side for each tray.

Job-site organization tips

Customized work carts

To save time, space and your back, here's a great way to organize and ferry everything you need for different jobs around the house. Use appliance dollies and bungee cords to create all-in-one carts. Make a compressor cart for nailing jobs, a saw cart with sawhorses on the back, and a cart of plastic crates loaded with supplies for wiring, painting and other common jobs. The carts make going up and down stairs easier, you don't have to drag along heavy tool cases and they really cut down the number of trips you make to and from the workshop.

Pencil keeper

If you don't wear a shirt with pockets, you may have a tough time keeping track of your carpenter's pencil. You can try sticking it behind your ear, but it won't stay there when you're wearing safety glasses. Here's the perfect solution—stick the pencil to your safety glasses with hook-and-loop tape.

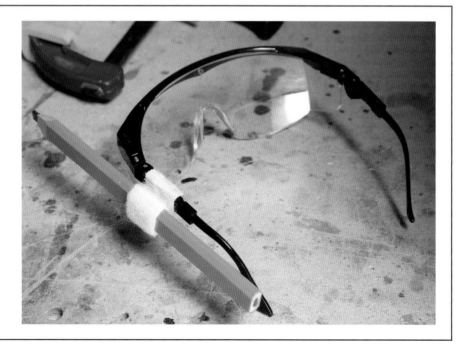

Crawl space helper

Crawl spaces can be a bit tight. So when you go "down under," try to make sure you have all your supplies with you to prevent multiple trips doing the military crawl to get stuff. One good solution is to load everything up in a concrete mixing pan and drag it along as you move around down there. An old plastic snow sled would work great too.

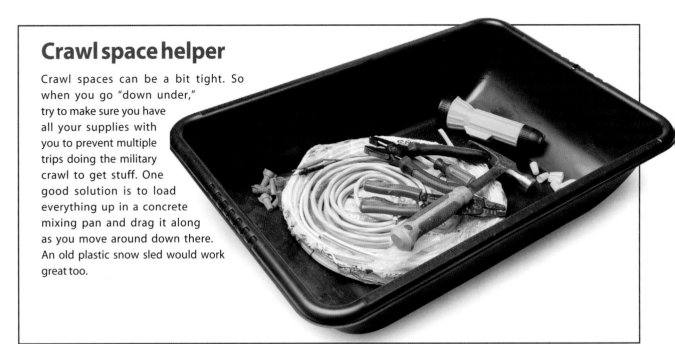

Bring extra fasteners

Dedicate a toolbox just for fasteners. You may think you'll need only two different size screws to finish your job, but it rarely works out that way. And keep a variety of bits along with the fasteners; that way you'll always have the right bit with the right screw.

Plastic-bag paint containers

If you paint your house using many colors, you'll probably find yourself constantly cleaning brushes and containers whenever you switch colors. A good way to make this easier is to put the paint in zipper lock bags. When it's time to change colors, all you do is change the bag in the paint bucket. It's a great way to save time and cleanup when you're using a lot of colors for a small paint job.

MAGNETIC KNIFE RACK

Ladder tool and screw holder

Here's a clever way to keep screws and tools handy when you're up on a ladder. Screw a magnetic tool holder or knife rack (available at home centers) to the top of your ladder. You don't have to worry about losing screws or knocking your screwdriver to the floor. Everything you need stays right where you put it.

Organize tools by the job

Knowing exactly which tools you'll need for every job is next to impossible. Organize your toolboxes and storage bins according to the work that needs to be done: a box for plumbing tools, electrical, drywall, etc. No doubt this will lead to owning more than one of the same tool. But you won't believe how much time you'll save having all the proper tools on hand.

Throw together a junk station

As soon as the major demo is completed, make yourself a junk station. Bring extra sawhorses, and throw a couple of boards or a piece of plywood on them. It's smart to have a central location for your tools, fasteners, batteries and chargers, radio, beverages and whatever else it takes to get the job done. Having items scattered all over the job-site floor makes cleanup harder, and wandering around looking for the stuff you need is a waste of time.

Space-saving workbench

Make your space work harder

A well-organized workshop with accessible storage and plenty of work space makes any project easier, but finding that space in a small garage can be a challenge. This workbench goes a long way toward solving that problem by simply making the space you have work harder. By combining a rollout workbench with a large work table and deep drawer bases, you can almost double the available work surface, plus make it easier to get at tools and put them away when you're done.

WHAT IT TAKES

Time: 2 weekends
Skill level: Intermediate

You can build the whole project with a circular saw and a drill, but a table saw, brad nailer, miter saw and router will make it go faster. The cost for lumber and hardware for this project is about $700 if you use maple plywood (as we did), or half that if you substitute standard BC-grade plywood. You can build the project in three to four days, with another day for applying finish.

Cut all the plywood first

The most time-consuming part of building the workbenches is ripping all the plywood parts. If you're working by yourself on a table saw, you may want to make the long rip cuts with a circular saw and a saw guide (for tips, search for "circular saw" at familyhandyman.com). Just make the shorter cuts on the table saw—it's difficult to muscle a 4 x 8-ft. sheet of plywood across a small saw bed without veering away from the fence. Label each piece as you cut it to avoid confusion later.

Assemble the bench

Attach the drawer slides to the drawer cabinet sides before you assemble the drawer bases (Photo 1). See Figure A p. 114 for placement. We used inexpensive 24-in. self-closing drawer slides that screw to the bottom edge of the drawer box. Side-mounted drawer slides require different placement.

Glue and clamp the drawer cabinet parts together, then predrill and screw them. Glue and nail the drawer cabinet cleats from the inside with 1-1/4-in. brad nails or screws.

Glue and screw a 2x4 to the edge of the plywood subtop, then clamp the subtop to the 1/2-in. plywood back. Attach both drawer cabinets (Photo 2), aligning them with the edges of the back and subtop—that will make the table square in both directions.

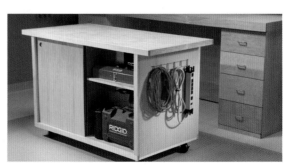
Long, deep drawers let you organize small tools, parts and hardware.

The rollout opens from both sides—one side for large tools, the other for small fasteners and supplies. Hooks at each end hold cords and hanging tools.

When you're done working, just tuck the rollout bench back under the fixed bench.

Tip the bench onto the floor and add the remaining 2x4s. Clamp the front 2x4 to a straightedge to keep the top flat, then glue and screw the 2x4s down. First screw them to the drawer cabinets with 2-1/2-in. screws (Photo 3), then finish by crawling under the bench and screwing the subtop to the 2x4s from underneath.

Finally, spread more glue on the 2x4s and set the plywood top into place. Fasten the top with finish nails, pushing down as you nail to make sure the plywood lies flat on the 2x4s. After the glue sets, the 2x4s and the plywood form a rigid structure called a torsion box, which will resist bending or sagging.

Build simple drawers

Build the drawer boxes 1 in. narrower than the opening (or as specified for the drawer slides you use). Attach the other half of the drawer slides to the boxes and set them into the drawer cabinets.

Position and fasten the drawer faces, then open the drawers and screw the faces to the drawer boxes from the inside with 1-1/4-in. screws (Photo 4). Use 16d nails or shims to create 1/8-in. gaps between the drawer faces.

Build the rollout bench

Using a router or a table saw with a dado blade, cut 1/4-in.-wide tracks for the sliding doors (Photo 5). Use an edge guide (make sure it's fastened tight) or clamp a straightedge to the plywood as a guide for the router. Cut the dadoes in the base first, then align it with the top and mark the cuts (the top and base are different widths). Cut the tracks in the base 3/16 in. deep and the tracks in the top 7/16 in. deep to make it easy to insert the sliding doors. Make the deeper router cuts in two passes. To help the doors slide easily, wrap 120-grit sandpaper around a small piece of 1/4-in. plywood and rub it back and forth in the door tracks to eliminate rough spots.

Center dividers make the bench strong

Glue and screw the 1x6 wheel supports (part X) to the edges of the base, then attach the casters with lag screws. Mark and drill matching shelf pin holes in the short center divider and the sides. Cut 3/4-in.-wide slots at the centers of the long and short dividers with the table saw (or circular saw) and jigsaw. Make the cuts 1/8 in. beyond the halfway marks so the two dividers will fit together easily and line up at the edges (Photo 6).

Position the dividers on the base as shown in Figure A, then lock them to the base with 3/4-in. cleats glued and nailed to the long divider. Set the sides into position on the 1x6 wheel supports and fasten them to the center divider and base with 1-1/2-in. brad nails (or screws if you don't mind seeing exposed screws).

Set the bottom layer of the benchtop into position, align the sides and the center divider, then tack everything into place with a few finish nails. Mark the centers of the dividers and sides, then predrill and screw the top down (Photo 7).

Spread glue over the top and fasten the second layer of the top with a finish nail at each corner. Then drive 1-1/4-in.

1 Save time and trouble by mounting drawer slides before assembling the cabinets. Lay the cabinet sides back-to-back, mark the slide locations and screw them into place.

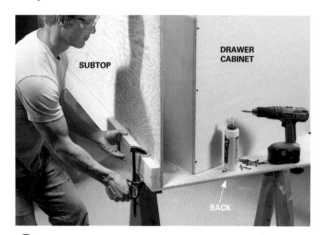

2 Join the back to the subtop with glue, screws and a 2x4, then glue and screw the drawer cabinets into place for a square, wobble-proof workbench.

3 Assemble a "sandwich" from 2x4s and plywood to form a super-stiff benchtop. Fasten 2x4s to the subtop, using clamps and a straightedge to hold the front edge flat. Then add the top layer of plywood.

Figure A
Workbench

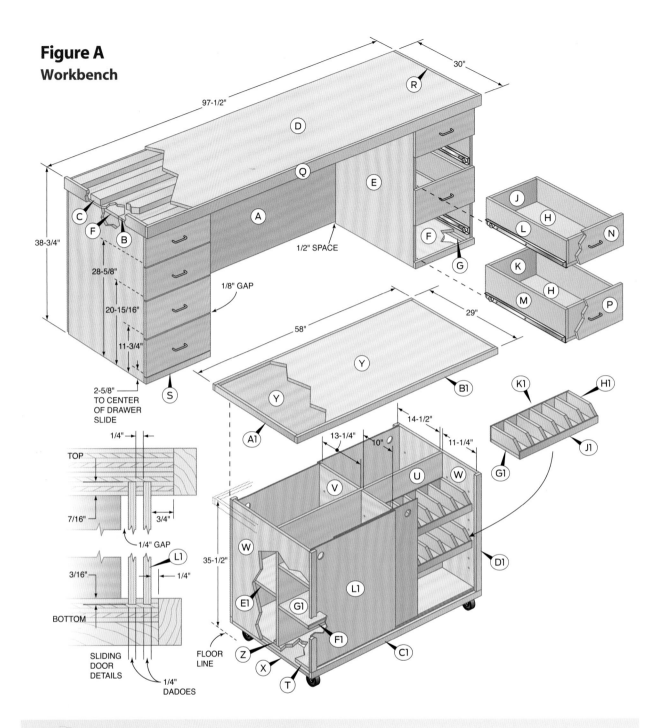

Materials list

(All materials are available from home centers or lumberyards)

ITEM	QTY.	ITEM	QTY.	ITEM	QTY
3/4" maple plywood	7	1x2 x 8' clear pine	5	1-1/4" nails for pneumatic finish nailer	
1/2" maple plywood	1	3/4" x 3/4" x 8' pine (rip from 1x2)	2		
1/2" BC-grade plywood	1	1/4" x 3/4" x 8' screen mold for shelf edging	3	3" locking casters	4
1/4" maple plywood	1			24" drawer slides	8 prs.
2x4 x 8'	4	Wood glue		Adjustable shelf pins	
1x6 x 6' pine	1	1-1/4" drywall screws		Drawer pulls	8
1x4 x 6' clear pine	1	1-5/8" drywall screws		1/4" x 1-1/4" lag screws (for wheels)	16
1x4 x 10' clear pine	1	2-1/2" drywall screw			

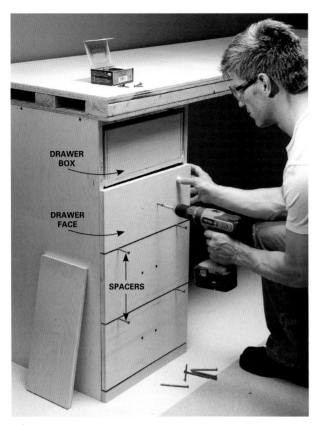

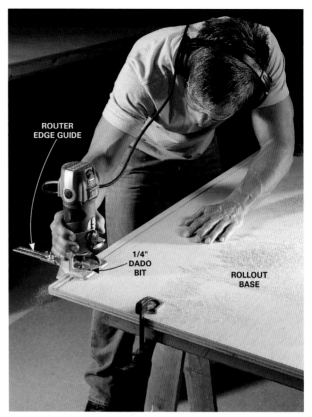

4 Position the drawer faces perfectly without guesswork by drilling holes for the handles and driving temporary screws through the holes. Then open each drawer and drive permanent screws from the inside.

5 Cut matching tracks for sliding doors in the benchtop and base before assembly. Use a straightedge or router guide to make the tracks perfectly straight.

Cutting list: Fixed workbench

KEY	PCS.	SIZE & DESCRIPTION
A	1	37-1/2" x 96" x 1/2" back
B	1	28-3/4" x 96" x 1/2" BC plywood subtop
C	4	2x4 x 96" studs
D	1	29-1/4" x 96" x 3/4" top
E	4	27-1/4" x 36" x 3/4" drawer cabinet sides
F	4	27-1/4" x 16-1/2" x 3/4" drawer cabinet tops and bottoms
G	4	27-1/4" x 3/4" x 3/4" pine drawer cabinet cleats
H	8	26" x 15-1/2" x 3/4" drawer box bases
J	8	14" x 5-3/4" x 3/4" drawer box fronts and backs
K	8	14" x 7-1/4" x 3/4" drawer box fronts and backs
L	8	26" x 5-3/4" x 3/4" drawer box sides
M	8	26" x 7-1/4" x 3/4" drawer box sides
N	4	18" x 7-13/16" x 3/4" drawer faces (for small drawers)
P	4	18" x 9" x 3/4" drawer faces (for large drawers)
Q	1	97-1/2" x 2-3/4" x 3/4" clear pine front trim
R	2	29-1/4" x 2-3/4" x 3/4" clear pine side trim

(All pieces are maple plywood unless noted.)

Cutting list: Rollout bench

KEY	PCS.	SIZE & DESCRIPTION
S	2	18" x 1-1/2" x 3/4" clear pine base trim
T	1	26-1/2" x 47-1/2" x 3/4" base
U	1	28-3/4" x 47-1/2" x 3/4" long center divider
V	1	28-3/4" x 24" x 3/4" short center divider
W	2	26-1/2" x 29-1/2" x 3/4" sides
X	2	26-1/2" x 3/4" x 5-1/2" pine wheel support
Y	2	27-1/2" x 56-1/2" x 3/4" top
Z	2	23-3/8" x 3/4" x 3/4" pine cleat
A1	2	27-1/2" x 1-1/2" x 3/4" clear pine trim
B1	2	58" x 1-1/2" x 3/4" clear pine trim
C1	2	49" x 1-1/2" x 3/4" clear pine base trim
D1	4	28-3/4" x 1-1/2" x 3/4" clear pine side trim
E1	4	13" x 23" x 3/4" plywood shelves
F1	6	23" x 1/4" x 3/4" shelf edge
G1	4	9-1/2" x 23" x 3/4" plywood shelves
H1	14	3" x 9-1/2" x 3/4" shelf dividers
J1	2	1-3/4" x 23" x 1/4" shelf front
K1	2	3-3/4" x 23" x 1/4" shelf back
L1	4	23-15/16" x 29-1/8" x 1/4" plywood door

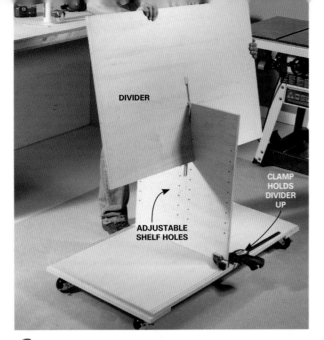

6 Leave the plywood dividers whole to create a sag-proof framework. Cut interlocking slots and then slide the dividers together and position them on the base.

Labels in image: DIVIDER, ADJUSTABLE SHELF HOLES, CLAMP HOLDS DIVIDER UP

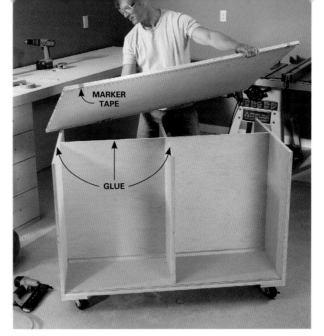

7 Mount the first layer of the benchtop, using masking tape markers to position it so you don't smear the glue. Then add the second layer of plywood to create a rock-solid surface.

Labels in image: MARKER TAPE, GLUE

8 Reinforce the cabinet by driving 1-5/8-in. screws through the base and wheel support into the dividers and sides.

Labels in image: CENTERLINES FOR SCREWS, 1-1/2", COUNTERSINK BIT

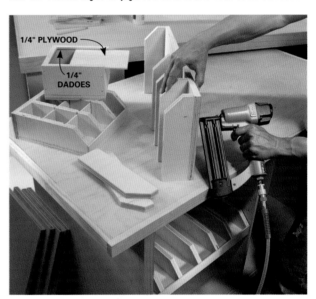

9 Don't let the leftovers go to waste! Build storage bins to fit inside the rollout bench. Use smaller pieces to make boxes for odds and ends.

Labels in image: 1/4" PLYWOOD, 1/4" DADOES

screws up through the bottom layer into the top to lock the two layers together.

Turn the rollout bench over and screw the base to the dividers and sides (Photo 8).

Doors, shelves and trim

Cut the doors for the rollout bench the height of the opening plus 3/8 in. so they can fit up into the top track and then drop into the bottom track without falling out. Cut holes for handles with a 1-1/2-in. hole saw. Back the doors with scrap wood before cutting the holes so they don't splinter. Rub hard paraffin wax (sold at hardware stores) along the bottom edges of the doors (after finish is applied) to make them slide smoothly in the tracks.

Add trim to both benches. Nail the upper and lower trim on the rollout bench to the outer edges only, to avoid nailing into the tracks. If desired, add 1/4-in. screen mold trim to finish the shelf edges. Sand all edges and rough spots on both workbenches.

Use the small pieces of leftover plywood to create bins on the shelves and storage containers for small parts and fasteners (Photo 9).

Finish the bench with either urethane varnish (durable but time-consuming to apply) or penetrating oil (goes on quickly but doesn't protect as well). Or leave it unfinished so you can accumulate a patina of marks and splatters from all the projects you make.

Shop organizing tips
from our Editors and readers

Bucket-lid blade holder

I got tired of my extra saw blades banging around in the drawer every time I opened it, so I attached them to a 5-gallon bucket lid with a bolt and a thumbscrew. Now they stay put, and the lid protects my hands when I'm digging around for other stuff.

Mark Petersen
TFH Contributing Editor

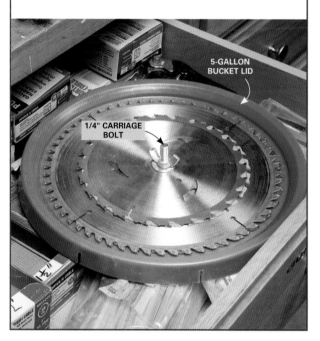

5-GALLON BUCKET LID

1/4" CARRIAGE BOLT

MAGNET

A safe chuck key holder

I used to hang the chuck key for my drill press on a string taped to the press. That worked well until the day I bumped it and the string caught the moving chuck and sent it flying. Luckily, it left an indentation in the wall instead of in me. Now I use a magnet to keep the chuck key handy—lesson learned.

Travis Larson
TFH Senior Editor

Tape measures always within reach

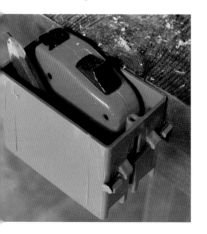

I have a dozen tape measures, but there was never one around when I needed it. So I bought a bunch of electrical junction boxes and nailed them up in strategic locations—next to the miter saw, the table saw, on my workbench, in the garden shed—and put a tape measure and pencil in each one. No more searching for a tape in the middle of a project.

Gary Wentz, TFH Senior Editor

In-line workshop

Place your planer, router table and radial arm saw all in a line and at the same height with roller stands on each end. This allows you to take a long piece of stock and cut, rout or plane it all on one worktable.

Reader photo

Build shallow drawers

I have a pretty organized shop with lots of drawers, and here's my tip. If you're going to build drawers, build lots of shallow ones and very few deep ones. Here's why. Just about everything you store for a shop is fairly thin—hand tools, blades, fasteners, sandpaper, etc. If you have a ton of shallow drawers, you can dedicate each one by category. Plus, it's easier to find what you need when it's not buried under 8 inches of other junk in the same drawer.

Travis Larson, *TFH* **Senior Editor**

Wire dispenser

A plastic crate is a great place to store anything on a spool. Just slip the spools onto a piece of metal conduit and secure the conduit with washers and bolts. There's even space below the spools for tools or scraps of wire.

Keep track of screw bits

It's common now for a box of screws to include a bit—for star or Torx heads, for example. But small bits always seem to disappear just when you need them. So next time you buy a box of screws, store them in a glass jar and glue a magnet to the inside of the lid. The magnet holds the bit, and you don't have to dump out all the screws to find it.

Extension cord smarts

To prevent tangled extension cords, use hook-and-loop tape to keep long cords organized. Wind the cord in 10-ft. loops and wrap each coil with hook-and-loop tape. That way you can easily unwrap only what you need for a given job. It keeps the work site safer and you don't have to unwind and rewind 50 ft. of cord when you only need 11.

HOOK-AND-LOOP TAPE

Sheet metal drawer liners

If you're one of those guys who uses old kitchen cabinets in your workshop, here's a tip for you. It's a bad idea to throw oily, greasy tools into those drawers, where the wood soaks up everything. Instead, take some careful measurements of the width, depth and height to any HVAC shop. For about $20 per drawer, you can get custom liners for each one. The interiors will look like new, and you'll be able to clean them as needed.

Utility trailer upgrades

WINCH STRAP

WINCH MOUNTED TO TONGUE

Most utility trailers come from the factory with just enough features to satisfy local safety regulations (if any) and your wallet. Sure, they work, but they're not very user-friendly. They rarely have factory tie-downs or holders or other features to make hauling easier. But your trailer doesn't have to stay that way. Here are some upgrades to make your trailer-hauling jobs a lot easier and safer. You can build and install most of the upgrades with just a socket set, drill, saw and screwdriver. Find the plumbing and hardware components at a home center or hardware store. Choose the upgrades you like.

Winch it in

Boat owners use a winch to pull their boat onto the trailer. You can install one on a utility trailer, too. It'll save your back and eliminate the need for a helper. Just wrap the strap around the heavy object and crank it up the ramp toward the front of the trailer. Bolt it to the trailer A-frame or tongue.

The plumber's trick

Ever tried to transport long or fragile items like pipe, drywall corner beads or drip edge? First you have to tie them in a bundle. Then you have

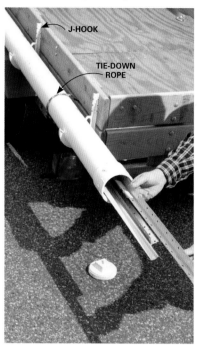

to secure the bundle to the trailer. Forget that! Instead, build the same kind of rig a plumber uses. Then just slide in the long items, screw on the cap, secure a red flag and you're good to go.

Buy a 10-ft. length of 4-in. PVC pipe, an end cap, a clean-out adapter, PVC cleaner and adhesive, and four J-hooks. Prime and glue the end cap and cleanout adapter. Take advantage of the wasted space on the side of your trailer and mount the tube there. Secure the four J-hooks to the side of the trailer and snap the tube into place. Tie the rig with rope for added security.

A cargo net and D-rings are great for "lighty, loosey" items

At highway speeds, light items can fly right out of your trailer. Even if they're tied down, they can break loose and take off. So you need one final mode of protection. We recommend a cargo net. Find one in the automotive section of the home center or at any auto parts store. Install D-rings every 18 in. along the top rails. You may be tempted to screw them into place. Don't. As the wood rails age, the screws can pull out. Instead, secure the D-rings with nuts and bolts. When you're finished loading, just throw the net over the trailer and clip the snaps to the rings.

7 ways to prevent trailer disasters

1 TIRES: Always replace trailer tires with "Special Trailer" (ST) tires (never passenger-rated tires). ST-rated tires have stronger sidewalls and are built to handle heavier loads. ST tires have a maximum life of five years from the date of manufacture. Replace yours accordingly.

2 TIRE PRESSURE: Inflate trailer tires to the pressure shown on the tire's sidewall. Or, if the sidewall pressure conflicts with the recommended pressure shown on the trailer manufacturer's nameplate, follow the manufacturer's pressure recommendation. Low tire pressure is the No. 1 cause of trailer tire failure. Overloading the trailer is No. 2.

3 LUG NUT/BOLT TORQUE: Tightening lug nuts or bolts to the proper torque is critical. If you're not using a torque wrench, you'll never get it right. The recommended torque should be listed on the trailer manufacturer's nameplate, and it's usually much higher than for cars and trucks. Never drive a loaded trailer with a missing lug nut or damaged lug bolt.

4 SAFETY CHAINS: Always cross the safety chains when you hook up to the hitch. The crossed chains catch the tongue and prevent it from hitting the pavement if it ever detaches from the receiver. Leave only enough chain slack to allow for turns. If your chain is longer than that, shorten it. Secure the coupler throw latch with a lock or clip to prevent it from popping open.

5 WHEEL BEARINGS: Failed wheel bearings are the No. 2 cause of all trailer breakdowns. Repack the bearings at least once a year (go to familyhandyman.com and search for "trailer" for a step-by-step article on repacking bearings). And don't pack the hub with grease. Extra grease in the hub generates heat that can cause premature bearing failure.

6 LOAD PLACEMENT: Place 60 percent of the weight toward the front of the trailer to prevent sway and fishtailing.

7 LUBRICATE THE BALL: If you don't, you're wearing out either the ball or the coupler. And that wear can cause a sudden and dangerous disconnect. Sure, grease is messy. But it's the only way to reduce heat and wear. Grease it or lose it.

CAP AND CHAIN

Vertical storage bins

Here's a great way to store your ratchet straps and bungee cords with the trailer, where they belong. Build vertical storage bins from 6-in. PVC pipe. Glue a cap on the bottom and drill a hole in it to overcome the suction when you pull off the lid. Then mount a handle on the top cap and attach a chain—perfect dry storage for whatever will fit inside.

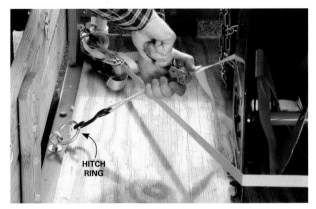

HITCH RING

Can't have too many tie-downs!

Did you know that poorly secured loads are responsible for more than 25,000 crashes and approximately 90 fatalities in this country each year? There's simply no such thing as too many tie-down anchors. Hitching rings work great for this. You can find them at most hardware stores. Buy at least six 3/8 x 5-1/8-in. hitching rings, and mount two each in the front, middle and near the tailgate. Just drill holes in the frame (not the floorboards), insert the long bolt end and secure the threaded portion with a locknut.

1-1/2" ELECTRICAL CONDUIT STRAP

The landscaper's trick

Landscapers and lawn care guys always haul around rakes, shovels, brooms and other implements by mounting vertical tubes on the front of their trailers. Here's our version. Cut 36-in. lengths of 1-1/2-in. PVC pipe and glue on an end cap. Then drill a hole in each end cap to provide drainage. Attach the tubes using PVC electrical conduit straps and nuts. If you plan to use the tubes in winter, secure them with metal straps—PVC gets brittle in cold weather and can shatter. For added security, hook a bungee strap to each implement.

Stow the spare

Flat tires are the No. 1 cause of trailer breakdowns. If you're not carrying a spare tire when you get a flat, you're in a heap of trouble. But where do you keep it—in the trailer bed where it's in the way? This spare tire carrier doesn't require assembly and can be mounted easily to the trailer rails. To lock the tire in place, simply run a bicycle locking cable down the tube and snap it shut.

A folding sawhorse with a built-in shelf

WHAT IT TAKES

Time: 1 hour each
Skill level: Beginner

Cut two blocks of wood to temporarily hold the shelf in place while you fasten the hinged side of the shelf to the legs.

Some horses have a shelf and some fold up, but this design combines both features. Plus, these horses are fun to build. To make a pair, you'll need a 4 x 4-ft. sheet of 3/4-in. plywood, one 8-ft. 2x6, one 8-ft. 2x4, two 12-ft. 2x4s and eight hinges.

Legs

After cutting the top 2x6 to length, cut both sides of each leg at a 15-degree angle. Make sure the angles are parallel. Fasten hinges to the ends of two of the legs, then attach those legs by fastening the hinges to the top piece. Attach the other two legs with 3-in. screws.

Shelf

Cut the 2x4 that supports one side of the shelf. Mark a line 8 in. up from the bottom of the leg, line up the bottom of the 2x4 with that line, and attach it with two 3-in. screws on each side. Cut the shelf to size and notch the two corners using a jigsaw. Fasten the hinges to the shelf, then use two 11-1/8-in. blocks of wood to temporarily hold the shelf in place while you fasten the hinged side of the shelf to the legs. Cut a 23-3/4-in. x 1-1/2-in. strip of plywood to overlap the 2x4 shelf brace. Attach it with wood glue and 1-1/4-in. screws. You may have to trim it a bit before fastening.

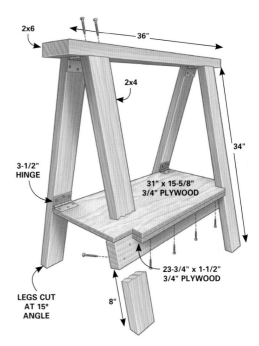

2x6

36"

2x4

34"

3-1/2" HINGE

31" x 15-5/8" 3/4" PLYWOOD

LEGS CUT AT 15° ANGLE

8"

23-3/4" x 1-1/2" 3/4" PLYWOOD

Keep track of stuff

Lawn chemical inventory

Do you find yourself buying duplicates of fungicides and weed killers because you can't remember what you already have? Or forgetting what they're for or how to use them all? One easy solution is to put all your lawn chemicals into a plastic bin, make a simple spreadsheet on the computer and attach it to the front of the bin. Now you can easily see what you have and how to use it.

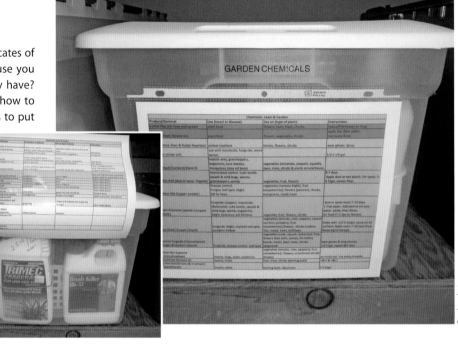

Reader photo

A picture is worth a thousand paint cans

Instead of dragging your paint can to the store to match the color, use a digital camera or your phone to snap a photo of the label. If you're really organized, you can snap a photo of all your paint can labels and keep a complete digital record of all your paint colors.

Keep paperwork on hand

If you find yourself ransacking the house to find paperwork related to your water heater, water softener and other mechanical systems, it's time to find a better way to store this important paperwork. One easy, effective solution is to use clear magnetic pouches (sold in various sizes at craft and office supply stores). They hold manuals, receipts and other paperwork, and you can stick them right onto the water heater, fridge, washer and dryer, and furnace. No more digging around for important papers.

7

Shelves & bookcases

3-tier basket stand

You've seen chests of drawers—well, here's a "chest of baskets." It can be used in nearly any room—but its small footprint makes it perfect for bathrooms with limited floor space. Use it for towels, hair dryers, extra toilet paper and anything else that fits.

The total materials bill for our pine stand, including the baskets, was about $50. We bought baskets at a craft store, but lots of other retailers such as Pier 1, West Elm and IKEA also carry them. Make sure to buy your baskets first; you need to construct the stand based on their dimensions.

To keep the frame of the stand both lightweight and strong, we used biscuit joinery. It's a clever way to join wood, and a technique you can use with many other projects. See p. 128 for biscuit joiner tips.

WHAT IT TAKES

Time: 4 hours
Skill level: Intermediate

EDGES OF RUNG AND
REAR CROSSPIECE

CENTER
OF BISCUIT

LEGS

1-1/2"

3/4"

EDGES OF
RUNNER

RUNG

LEG

Bill Zuehlke (5 photos this page)

1 Mark the legs. Clamp the legs together and mark them all at the same time. That way, all your marks will line up and you'll avoid mismatches.

2 Cut the biscuit slots. Cut slots in the ends of the rungs and sides of the legs. Assemble each ladder in a "dry run" to make sure they fit together correctly.

3 Assemble the "ladders." Join the rungs to the legs with glue and biscuits, then clamp the ladders together. Work fast! You have to assemble eight joints before the glue begins to set.

How to build it

You'll build the two "ladders" that form the sides of the stand, then glue and nail the crosspieces to join the two ladders.

To get started, cut all the parts to length (see Cutting List, p. 128). Mark the rung and crosspiece locations on the legs. Mark all four legs at the same time to ensure the framework is uniform and square (Photo 1).

As you mark the legs, keep picturing how your baskets will sit on the runners, especially if you're using baskets smaller or larger than ours; it will help you avoid mental errors. Use the biscuit joiner to cut slots in the edges of the legs and ends of the rungs (Photo 2). You'll need to clip the biscuits to suit the 1-1/2-in.-wide legs and rungs (see p. 128).

Apply glue to the biscuits and slots (Photo 3) and assemble each joint. Clamp the ladders together and set them aside until the glue dries.

Join the two ladders by gluing and nailing the crosspieces between them. Remember that the three front crosspieces that will support the baskets lie flat. Next, install the basket runners (Photo 4) even with the flat crosspieces that run across the front. Glue and nail the 3/4-in. plywood top to the stand, then apply cove molding to cover the edges (Photo 5).

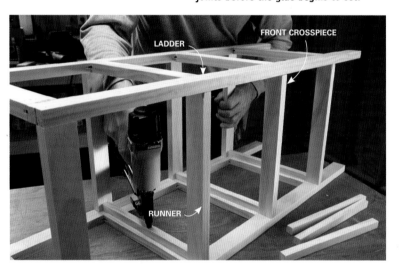

LADDER

FRONT CROSSPIECE

RUNNER

4 Connect the ladders. Install the front and back crosspieces with glue and nails. Then add the runners that support the baskets.

PLYWOOD TOP

COVE MOLDING

5 Top it off. Glue and nail the plywood top to the top of the stand, then apply cove molding to neaten up and hide the edges.

Figure A
Basket stand

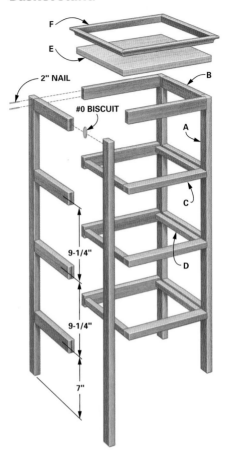

F

E

2" NAIL

B

#0 BISCUIT

A

9-1/4"

C

9-1/4"

D

7"

Overall Dimensions:
14-1/2" x 15-1/4" x 36-3/4"

Materials list

Here's what we used to make this basket stand: 30 ft. of 1x2, 6 ft. of 3/4-in. x 3/4-in. square dowel, 6 ft. of 3/4-in. cove molding, 3/4-in. plywood, 12 x 12 x 8-in. baskets, No. 0 biscuits, wood glue, 2-in. finish nails, penetrating oil cherry finish.

Cutting list

KEY	PCS.	SIZE & DESCRIPTION
A	4	3/4" x 1-1/2" x 36" legs
B	8	3/4" x 1-1/2" x 10" rungs
C	8	3/4" x 1-1/2" x 12-1/4" crosspieces
D	6	3/4" x 3/4" x 10-3/4" runners
E	1	3/4" x 13" x 13-3/4" top
F	4	3/4" cove molding (cut to fit)

Using biscuit joiners

A biscuit joiner is a superb tool for joining wood where it would be difficult to use nails or screws. The joint is strong, invisible and easy to create. The compressed wood biscuits expand on contact with moisture in the glue. Since the biscuits are placed in slots that are wider than the biscuit, you can adjust the joint a little after butting the two pieces together. Biscuits come in three common sizes: No. 0, No. 10 and No. 20. Whether you're building this basket stand or some other biscuit project, here are some of our favorite biscuit tips:

Clip biscuits for narrow stock

The smallest common biscuits (No. 0) are almost 1-7/8 in. long. That's too long for the 1-1/2-in. wide parts on this basket stand. But there's an easy solution: Just clip about 1/4 in. off both ends of each biscuit. Your slots will still be too long and visible at inside corners, but a little filler and finish will hide them.

Number the joints

While you're marking the center lines of each biscuit slot, also number each joint. That will eliminate confusion and misalignments during assembly.

Make a glue injector

Spreading a neat, even bead of glue inside a biscuit slot isn't easy. You can buy special injectors online, or make your own using the cap from a marker and a fine-tooth saw.

Always do a dry run

Biscuits grab fast. During glue-up, you don't have time to correct mistakes or dig up a longer set of clamps. So always test the whole assembly—including clamps—before you get out the glue. For complicated assemblies, give yourself more working time by using slow-setting wood glue.

Super-simple DVD holder

This clever shelf holds DVDs, CDs or even small books. You can make yours with as many shelves as you like simply by changing the length of the trunk.

To get started, cut the trunk and shelves to length. Bevel one end of each shelf by tilting your miter saw or table saw blade to 5 degrees. Mark the notches in the shelves and trunk (Photos 1 and 2). Measuring from the top of the trunk, center the notches at 8-1/2, 11-1/2, 17-1/4, 20-1/4, 26-1/4 and 29 in. Cut the notches using a 5-degree guide block and a pull saw (available at home centers). Assemble the shelf (Photo 3). Screw metal straps to the back of the trunk, leaving one screw hole exposed so you can screw the DVD holder to the wall.

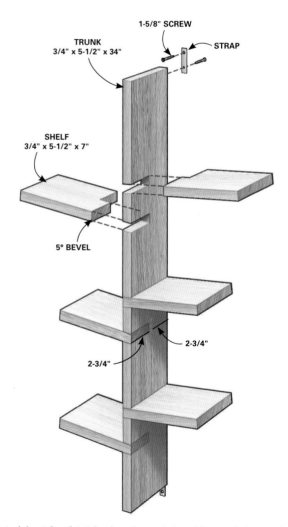

1-5/8" SCREW
TRUNK
3/4" x 5-1/2" x 34"
STRAP
SHELF
3/4" x 5-1/2" x 7"
5° BEVEL
2-3/4"
2-3/4"

Materials: 8 ft. of 1x6 hardwood, wood glue, 2-in. x 1/2-in. metal straps, 1-5/8-in. screws, spray lacquer.

BEVEL GAUGE
MITER GAUGE

1 Set your bevel gauge at 5 degrees using the miter gauge and fence of your table saw.

BEVEL GAUGE
TRUNK
SHELF

2 Mark the notches on the edge of the trunk using the bevel gauge. Mark the face of the trunk with a square.

3 Test-fit each shelf and then glue it into place. If a shelf fits so tightly that it's hard to remove after test-fitting, just leave it—no glue is needed.

WHAT IT TAKES

Time: 2 hours
Skill level: Intermediate

Leaning tower of shelves

This stylish but sturdy shelf unit will neatly hold your stuff

This shelf unit may look lightweight and easy to topple. But don't be fooled. It's a real workhorse. The 33-1/2-in. x 82-3/4-in. tower features five unique, tray-like shelves of different depths to hold a wide variety of items up to 13-1/4 in. tall. Despite its 10-degree lean, the unit is surprisingly sturdy, and its open design won't overpower a room. Whether you choose to make this piece more functional, as in this office setting, or place it in a family room to showcase treasures, the basic construction is the same. Select the type of wood and stain or paint to dress it up (or down) to fit the look of any room.

All the materials can be purchased at home centers or lumberyards. The only special tools you'll need are a power miter saw for crisp angle cuts and a brad nailer for quick assembly and almost invisible joints. And you'll have to rustle up an old clothes iron for applying oak edge-banding. Once you've gathered all the material, you can build the shelf unit in one afternoon.

Buying the wood

This unit was built with red oak and oak veneer plywood and finished with two coats of red oak stain. The beauty of this project is that any wood species will work. If you plan to paint it, select alder or aspen for the solid parts and birch for the plywood.

One note when buying boards: Use a tape measure to check the "standard" dimensions of 1x3s and 1x4s. They sometimes vary in width and thickness. Also check the two full-length 1x4s you plan to use as the uprights to be sure they're straight, without warps or twists. And always examine the ends, edges and surface for blemishes or rough areas that won't easily sand out.

WHAT IT TAKES

Time: 1 day
Skill level: Beginner

Figure A Modular shelf assembly

1x4 x 14-1/2"
CLEAT F

1x3

1x3

SHELF A

3-3/8"

4-3/8"

SHELF B

5-3/4"

6-3/4"

CLEAT G
1x4 x 11-3/4"

11-3/4"

8-3/16"

SHELF C

9-3/16"

F

J

G

G

G

G

1x4 x 84"
UPRIGHT

10-5/8"

SHELF D

11-5/8"

30-1/2"   13"

SHELF E   14"

CLEAT H
1x4 x 10"

H

CUT CLEAT
ENDS
AT 10°

Figure B
Top of upright

2-1/32"

8-3/8"

F
AND
J

10° ANGLE

Materials list

- One half-sheet (4' x 4') of 3/4" oak plywood
- Three 8' oak 1x3s
- Four 8' oak 1x4s
- One package (25') of 7/8" oak iron-on veneer (available at home centers)
- Veneer edge trimmer
- Wood glue
- 1-1/4" brad nails
- Foam pads (3/4" round, self-adhesive non-skid pads)

Cutting list

QTY.	SIZE & DESCRIPTION
1	3/4" x 3-3/8" x 30-1/2" oak plywood (shelf A base)
1	3/4" x 5-3/4" x 30-1/2" oak plywood (shelf B base)
1	3/4" x 8-3/16" x 30-1/2" oak plywood (shelf C base)
1	3/4" x 10-5/8" x 30-1/2" oak plywood (shelf D base)
1	3/4" x 13" x 30-1/2" oak plywood (shelf E base)
2	3/4" x 2-1/2" x 4-3/8" oak (shelf A sides)*
2	3/4" x 2-1/2" x 6-3/4" oak (shelf B sides)*
2	3/4" x 2-1/2" x 9-3/16" oak (shelf C sides)*
2	3/4" x 2-1/2" x 11-5/8" oak (shelf D sides)*
2	3/4" x 2-1/2" x 14" oak (shelf E sides)*
5	3/4" x 2-1/2" x 30-1/2" oak A–E (shelf backs)
2	3/4" x 3-1/2" x 14-1/2" oak shelf cleats F (cut with 10-degree angles)
8	3/4" x 3-1/2" x 11-3/4" oak shelf cleats G (cut with 10-degree angles)
2	3/4" x 3-1/2" x 10" oak shelf cleats H (cut with 10-degree angles)
2	3/4" x 3-1/2" x 84" oak uprights J (cut with 10-degree angles)

Front part of side cut at 10 degrees.

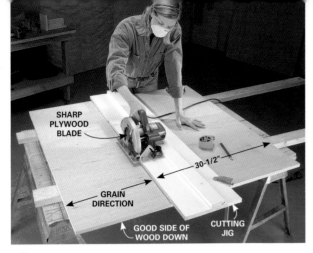

1 Cut 3/4-in. shelf plywood to width first, using a circular saw and a homemade jig for exact cuts. Use a sharp plywood blade and cut with the best side of the wood facing down to minimize splintering.

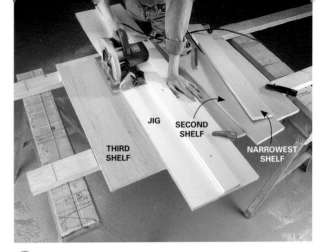

2 Cut the individual shelves, beginning with the narrowest, using the jig for perfectly straight cuts.

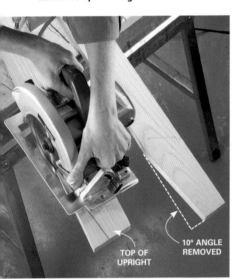

3 Cut both shelf uprights to length with a miter saw. Clamp to sawhorses. Mark the 10-degree angle at the top (dimensions in Figure B), then cut with a circular saw.

4 Iron edge-banding veneer to the front edge of all five shelves. Roll the entire surface to ensure a solid bond, and trim the edges.

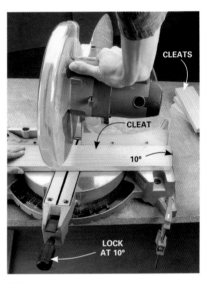

5 To maintain accuracy, lock the miter box at 10 degrees, then cut all angled pieces—uprights, cleats and one end of shelf sides—without changing the table.

Cut plywood shelves first

Lay a couple of 2x4s across sawhorses (Photo 1) to cut the half sheet of 3/4-in. plywood cleanly and without pinching the saw blade. Since all five shelves are 30-1/2 in. wide, cut this width first, making sure the grain will run the long way across the shelves. Remember to wear safety glasses, earplugs and a dust mask. Make a homemade jig to fit your circular saw and clamp it to the plywood.

Next, cut all five shelf depths, starting with the smallest shelf (3-3/8 in.) first. Cut smallest to largest so you'll have enough wood to clamp the jig. **Important:** Make sure you account for the width of your saw blade when you cut each shelf.

Now mark and cut the top of all four 1x4 uprights (the end that rests against the wall), according to Photo 3 and the two dimensions provided in Figure B. Use a sharp blade in your circular saw to prevent splintering.

Select the best front of each plywood shelf, clamp it to the bench on edge and sand it smooth with 150-grit paper on a sanding block. Then preheat a clothes iron to the "cotton" setting and run it over the top of the edge-banding veneer, making sure the veneer extends beyond all edges (Photo 4). Roll it smooth immediately after heating. Let each shelf edge cool for a couple of minutes before trimming and sanding the edges.

Cut the uprights and shelf frame

Now enter the miter saw, which you use to make all the 90-degree straight cuts first (five shelf backs and 10 shelf sides; see Cutting List). **Important:** Remember that one end of each shelf side has a 10-degree cut, so first cut them square at their exact length, then cut the angle carefully so the long edge of each piece remains the same.

Next, rotate the miter saw table to the 10-degree mark and cut all the angle pieces. First cut the bottom of both uprights so each upright rests flat against the floor and wall (see Figure A). Then trim the top of the upright to match the bottom,

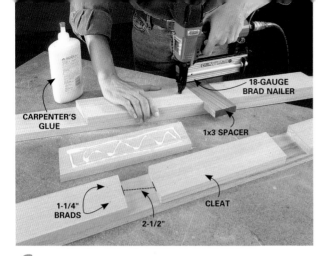

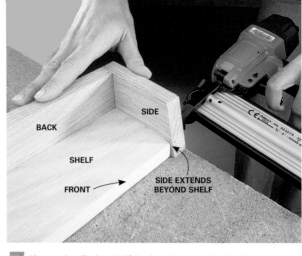

6 Glue and nail the shelf cleats to the uprights using a 1x3 spacer. Hold each cleat tight to the spacer.

7 Glue and nail the shelf backs, then attach the sides to the plywood shelves. Position the sides to overlap the shelf base as shown.

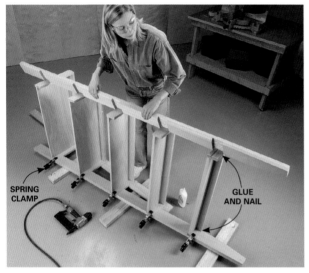

9 Set the shelf unit against a straight wall, check for square-ness and apply three bar clamps until the glue dries.

8 Clamp the shelves into one upright. Spread glue in the shelf notches of the other upright, position it flush with the front of the shelves and nail. Flip the unit over and attach the other upright.

being careful to maintain the 84-in. total length. Next, cut the cleats based on the Cutting List dimensions, which are measured edge to edge (Photo 5 and Figure A). Leave the top cleats long and cut them to exact fit during assembly. Then, to speed finishing, use an orbital sander with 150-grit sandpaper to smooth all pieces before assembly.

Assemble uprights first, then the shelves

To begin assembly, lay out both uprights and all cleats to ensure that the angles are correct so the shelves will be level when the unit is against the wall. Then glue and nail the first cleat flush with the base of each upright (using five or six 1-1/4-in. brads) on each cleat. Work your way upward using 1x3 spacers (Photo 6). Make sure the spacer is the exact same width as the shelf sides! Set these aside to dry.

For shelf assembly, first glue and nail on the shelf backs. Next, apply the sides with glue and nails (Photo 7).

For final assembly, lay one upright on 2x4s, then clamp on the shelves as shown in Photo 8. Apply the glue, position the second upright on top flush with the front edge of the shelves, then sink four 1-1/4-in. brads into each shelf from the upright side. Carefully turn the unit over and repeat the process to attach the second upright. Work quickly so the glue doesn't set. Lift the ladder shelf and place it upright against a straight wall. Check it with a framing square and flex it if necessary to square it up and to make sure that the uprights rest flat against the floor and wall (assuming your floor is level). Attach three bar clamps as shown in Photo 9 while the glue dries.

The shelf is highly stable as designed, but once you've stained or painted it, you can add self-adhesive foam gripping pads to the bottom of the uprights. And if you don't feel secure having it on a slippery floor, the unit's width is perfect for screwing the top of the uprights into wall studs.

Hanging shelves

From leveling to anchoring, here are 10 tips to make sure your next shelf-hanging project is quick, easy and strong. We'll show you tips for hanging and installing everything from store-bought display shelves to DIY closet shelves. And even if you don't have any shelf projects in the near future, you'll find leveling and anchoring tips here that you can use on other building projects.

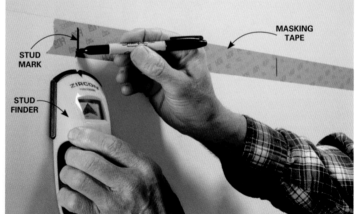

STUD MARK

STUD FINDER

MASKING TAPE

1 Mark the tape, not the wall

The first step in any shelf-hanging project is to locate the studs so you can anchor the shelf to the studs if possible. Here's a tip that allows you to make marks that are clearly visible without the need to repaint the wall.

Use a level and draw a very light pencil line where you want the top of the shelf to be. The shelf will hide the line. Apply a strip of masking tape above the line. Use "delicate surface" masking tape to avoid any possibility of messing up the paint. Locate the studs and mark the centers on the tape. Electronic stud finders are the go-to tool for this task. Now you can plan your shelf-mounting project to hit as many studs as possible and use the tape as a guide for leveling and attaching the shelf.

2 Figure-eights simplify the job

These nifty little fasteners are actually designed to attach table and desktops to aprons (the vertical skirt around the perimeter), but they're also a handy solution for hanging shelves. You can buy a pack of eight at woodworking stores or online.

The only caveat is that the top of the figure-eight shows above the surface of the shelf, so it may be visible if you hang the shelf low. Try to position the figure-eights where there are studs. You can use good-quality hollow-wall anchors if the studs don't line up with the figure-eights.

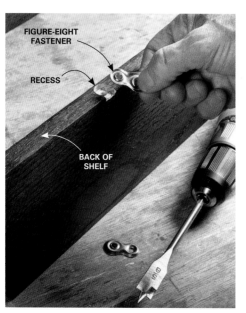

FIGURE-EIGHT FASTENER

RECESS

BACK OF SHELF

Drill a recess for the figure-eight
Use a spade bit or Forstner bit to drill a slight recess in the back of the shelf to accommodate the thickness of the figure-eight. Then chisel out the remaining wood until the figure-eight sits flush to the shelf. Attach the figure-eight with a screw.

Simply screw it on
Mount the shelf by driving screws through the figure-eights either into hollow-wall anchors or into studs.

SHELF LEVEL

LASER LINE

SELF-LEVELING LASER

3 Dead-on leveling with a laser

Got a lot of shelves to level? A laser level is the perfect tool. We're using a self-leveling laser, but any laser that projects a horizontal level line will work. The tip is that you don't have to mess with getting the laser line at the height of your shelf. Just project it anywhere on the wall, and use it as a reference by measuring up from the line. This is especially handy if you're mounting several shelves at different heights, since you never need to reposition the laser. You can pick up a self-leveling laser for under $50 and use it for many other interior leveling tasks.

4 Super-sturdy closet shelves

Here's a fast, strong and easy way to install closet shelves. Paint a 1x4 to match your shelf. Then draw a level line and locate the studs or use our masking tape trick (p. 134). Nail the 1x4 to the studs with 8d finish nails. Run the strip across the back and ends of the closet. Then put blocks in the locations where you want brackets. Now you have solid wood to attach the brackets and the closet pole sockets to. And the back of the shelf is fully supported to prevent sagging.

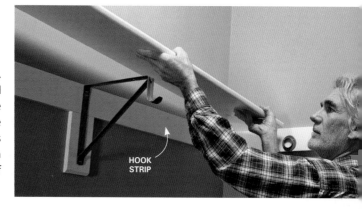

HOOK STRIP

LOW-QUALITY
FREE ANCHOR

NOTCHED
BRACKET

HANGING
RAIL

5 Throw away the free anchors

Most of the hollow-wall anchors included with shelves or shelf brackets aren't worth using. If you can't attach your shelf to studs and must use hollow-wall anchors, make sure to choose one that will support your shelf in the long run.

For light-duty shelves, we like the type of anchor shown here. You'll find them at any hardware store or home center. Make sure you know how thick your drywall or plaster is before you head to the store, though. Then match the anchor to the wall thickness.

To install the anchors, check the instructions and drill the right size hole. Then fold the wings so the anchor will fit and press it into the hole. You may have to tap it with a hammer until it's fully seated. Finish by pressing the included red tool through the hole to expand the wings behind the drywall or plaster. And make sure to use the screws included with the anchors, or ones that are the same diameter.

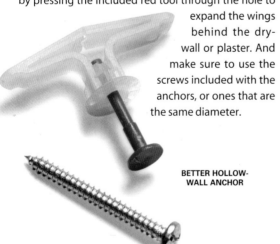

BETTER HOLLOW-
WALL ANCHOR

6 Build in a hanging rail

Whether you're building a shelf or modifying a store-bought unit, including a hanging rail is a great way to add strength and allow for more flexible positioning while anchoring to studs. The rail strengthens the shelf and lets you anchor the shelf by driving screws anywhere along the length of the rail.

If the shelf isn't too heavy, you can hang it with finish-head screws that are easy to hide with wood putty. For heavier shelves, drill recesses for wood plugs to hide the screws.

7 Self-plumbing standards

LOOSE
SCREW

SHELF
STANDARD

The next time you install metal shelf standards, remember this tip. Rather than use a level to plumb the standards before you attach them, simply hang them loosely from the top with one of the screws and let gravity do the work. The standard will hang plumb, and all you have to do is press it to the wall and drive in the remaining screws. If you're using hollow-wall anchors, hang the standard from the top screw and use an awl to mark the screw locations. Then take the standard down and install the anchors.

8 The key to keyholes

Keyhole slots on the back of shelves are a common way to hang shelves or brackets on hidden screws, but you have to get the screws perfectly aligned or you'll have all kinds of trouble.

Here's one foolproof method for transferring a pair of keyhole locations to the wall for perfect screw placement. If you're lucky, you may be able to line up the screw locations with studs. Otherwise, use this method to mark the center of the hollow-wall anchors you'll need.

MASKING TAPE

KEYHOLE HANGER

Mark; don't measure
Place a strip of masking tape on one edge of your level and mark the center of each keyhole on the tape.

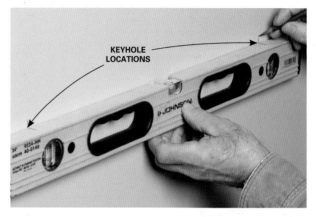

KEYHOLE LOCATIONS

Transfer to the wall
Hold the level against the wall at the height you want the shelf. Remember that the top of the shelf will be above your marks. Adjust the level until the bubble is centered, and mark the keyhole locations on the wall. Then install anchors or drive the screws into the studs and hang the shelf.

9 A better anchor for heavy shelves

Of course it's always best to fasten heavy shelves to studs, but if you can't, there's an anchor that's almost as good. If you've used standard toggle bolts, you know they hold well. But they're a hassle to work with, and they leave an oversize hole that may show. And if you ever need to take the shelf down to paint, the toggle falls into the wall and you have to repeat the whole tedious process when you reinstall the shelf.

TOGGLE BOLT

Snaptoggle anchors solve these problems. After installing the toggle according to the instructions, you'll have a threaded opening in the wall ready to receive the included bolt. You can simply screw the shelf to the captured toggle. And you can remove the bolt and the toggle will stay put, ready for you to reinstall the shelf. You'll find snaptoggle anchors in hardware stores and home centers alongside the other wall anchors.

SNAPTOGGLE ANCHOR

10 French cleats for fast, solid hanging

Pairs of beveled strips that interlock to support shelves, cabinets or pictures are called French cleats. They're great for hanging any shelf or cabinet and have a few advantages in certain situations.

First, the cleats work well for heavy cabinets because you can easily mount the wall cleat and then simply lift the cabinet and "hook" it on. There's no need to support a heavy cabinet temporarily while you drive screws to anchor it.

Another common use for French cleats is to create a flexible system of shelves or cabinets. You can screw one or more lengths of wall cleats across the entire wall, and then easily relocate shelves, or add more shelves at a later date. Make cleats by ripping strips of 3/4-in. plywood with a 45-degree bevel on one edge. Screw one strip to the wall and the other to the back of the shelf or cabinet.

SHELF CLEAT

WALL CLEAT

FLAT-SCREEN TV
bookcase

Traditional style designed for high-tech entertainment

WHAT IT TAKES — **Time:** 3 weekends — **Skill level:** Advanced

Television image: © Wisconsinart | Dreamstime.com • Illustration FRANK ROHRBACH III

Until recently, it was hard to pack a high-quality sound system and TV into a traditional bookcase. Today's smaller systems finally let you combine big sight and sound with classic design.

You don't need a huge shop or industrial equipment to build this bookcase. We'll show you how to cut and machine plywood perfectly without a pro-grade table saw. If your shop has enough open space to lay a sheet of plywood on sawhorses, then it's big enough for this project. Plus, you won't have to wrestle full sheets of plywood across the table saw. If you've been thinking about buying a new router, now is the time—this project will give it a good workout.

This bookcase will accommodate most 42-in. flat screen TVs, but not all. So make sure to measure your TV before you build. The total materials bill for this entertainment center—built from cherry—was about $1,250. Using less costly wood, such as oak, would cut the cost by about $400. This building method requires four different router bits. If you don't already own them, expect to spend a bit more.

Slice up the plywood

Rough-cut plywood with a circular saw and then clean up the cuts with a router. That gives me perfectly smooth, straight, splinter-free cuts and lets me skip the struggle of steering full sheets across the table saw.

Mark out your cuts following the cutting diagrams on p. 144, then rough-cut (Photo 1). Keep the rough cuts at least 1/8 in. from the cutting line. Don't worry about getting a perfectly square cut at this point—close counts. Be sure to keep the pairs of parts A, D, B and E together so you can dado them in one pass (Photo 3) and later cut them apart. Don't forget to leave a little extra width on these grouped sections to accommodate saw cuts.

Finish the rough cuts with a router and a pattern bit (Photo 2). Set the straightedge against the line, clamp and rout. For shorter pieces such as shelves, rough-cut with the circular saw, finish the cut on one end with the router, then cut to final length on the table saw.

Cut the dadoes

Plywood has a good side and a not-so-good side. Keep this in mind when you lay out your dadoes. You want the best face turned toward the outside of the cabinets.

Lay out the dadoes using a square and a straightedge. Be sure to mark an "X" or two alongside the line where the dado goes. If you forget to do this, you'll eventually run a dado on the wrong side of the line.

TIP:
Trim 1/2 in. off the plywood's factory edges to remove nicks and dents from handling.

You can cut the dadoes with a standard 3/4-in. bit, but it's better to use a special 23/32-in. "plywood" bit, which matches the actual thickness of so-called 3/4-in. plywood. You'll need to add a bearing and stop collar to a plywood bit. Unfortunately, a 3/4-in. bearing is as close as you can get to the 23/32-in. plywood bit. This creates a tiny, 1/64-in. offset, an amount so slight you can ignore it. The measurements for shelf placement are not that critical.

Cut dadoes in the bookcase sides and the two dividers (Photo 3). Then split the paired parts by ripping them on the table saw. Before doing any other machining, dry-fit the lower half of the center bookcase (including the dividers, drawer runners, middle and bottom shelves and sides) to make sure all your pieces fit properly. This is a good time to cut the edging for the drawer runners and dividers. Glue and clamp these while the lower half is dry-fitted together. After the glue has set, disassemble and sand the hardwood edges flush to the veneer.

Next, cut 1/4-in. x 3/8-in. rabbets in the bookcase sides (Photo 4). These grooves create a recess for the 1/4-in. plywood backs. Finally, cut the shelf standard slots with a router and a 5/8-in. top-bearing mortise bit (Photo 5). It's better to use a router rather than a dado blade in your table saw. It's a lot harder to get a consistent groove depth on a table saw because you're forced to keep a long bookcase side flat on the table while feeding it over the dado blade.

Glue hardwood skids onto the bottom edge of each bookcase side and toe board. The skids protect the delicate veneer from catching and tearing when the cabinets are moved. Sand the edging flush.

1 Rough-cut the plywood. Keep the saw blade at least 1/8 in. from the cutting line so you can trim the plywood to final size later. Don't cut the cabinet sides apart until you've cut the dadoes (Photo 3).

CABINET SIDES

2 Trim rough edges smooth. Clean up the saw cuts with a pattern bit and a straightedge. Take your time to position the straightedge for a perfectly square cut.

PATTERN BIT

CLEAN, CRISP EDGE

ROUGH-CUT EDGE

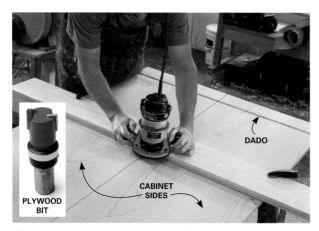

3 Dado two sides at once. Cut the shelf dadoes with a plywood bit, which matches the thickness of the plywood. Then cut the cabinet sides apart and you'll have perfectly matched dadoes.

PLYWOOD BIT

DADO

CABINET SIDES

4 Rabbet the back edges. Cut the rabbets for the backs with a rabbeting bit. There's no need for a straightedge here; the bearing rides right on the plywood edge.

RABBETING BIT

RABBET

Figure A
Exploded view

Overall dimensions:
115" W x 17" D x 86" H

A lift-off lid turns the center crown into a secret storage compartment.

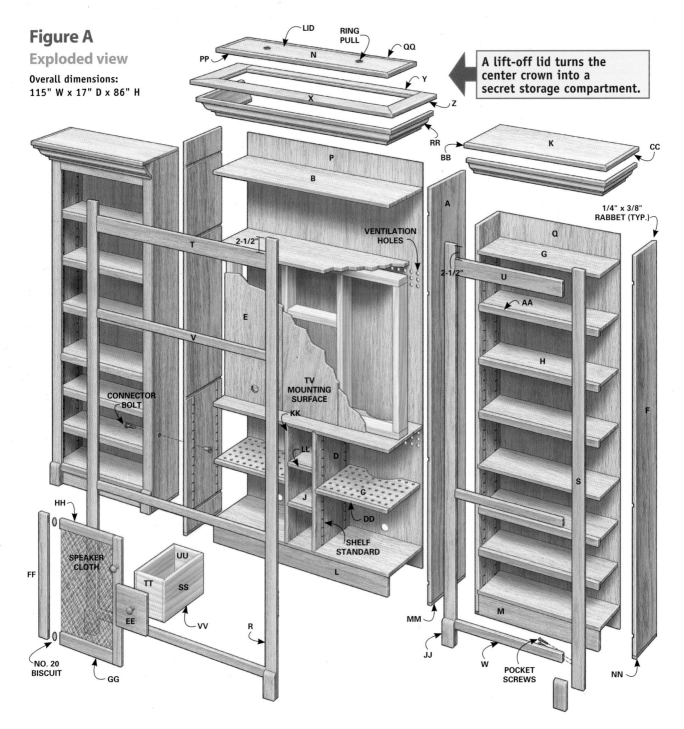

1/4" x 3/8" RABBET (TYP.)

VENTILATION HOLES

TV MOUNTING SURFACE

CONNECTOR BOLT

SHELF STANDARD

SPEAKER CLOTH

NO. 20 BISCUIT

POCKET SCREWS

Prefinish to save time

Cherry is hard to stain evenly, so we skipped the stain and finished the bookcase with three coats of oil-based poly.

Apply all but the final coat on the interior (Photo 6). Prefinishing lets you work on flat horizontal surfaces. It's much easier than brushing into the back of a cabinet with all those corners or working on the underside of a shelf. Best of all, it prevents sags and drips.

Use painter's tape to line the dadoes and tape off the front edge where the face frame attaches. Brush on two coats of poly, sanding between coats. When you sand the second coat, skip the underside of the fixed shelves. These nonwear areas need only two coats.

The dry fit

Now it's time to dry-fit the entire bookcase. The dry fit is a dress rehearsal. It lets you discover problems, work out clamping strategies and avoid disasters. (It's no coincidence that "glue-up" rhymes with "screw-up.") Start from the inside of the big cabinet with the drawer runners and dividers. Add the shelves on the top and bottom of the dividers and work your way out. Use screws wherever an adjoining cabinet will later hide them. Screws are easier and faster than clamps.

Once all three cabinets are dry-fitted, stand them up and clamp them together, making sure the backs line up flush. Bore the holes for the connector bolts (Photo 7). Use four bolts along the front edges and two in the back.

5 Cut grooves for the shelf supports. Rout shallow dadoes with a mortising bit. Center the bit in the shelf dado before you turn on the router. Shelf standards recessed in a dado look neater than surface-mounted standards.

6 Start your finish. Finishing the insides of the cabinets is a lot easier before assembly. Keep the polyurethane off the surfaces that will be glued later. Glue won't stick to poly.

7 Bolt the cabinets together. Clamp the cabinets together and drill holes for the connector bolts. Be sure the backs line up flush and use a backer board to prevent blowout where the bit exits.

Materials list

ITEM	QTY
4' x 8' x 3/4" cherry plywood	5
4' x 8' x 1/4" cherry plywood	3
4' x 8' x 1/2" multi-ply birch plywood	1/4
Cherry hardwood (board feet)	35

Hardware*

Cast steel classic knobs	5
3/4" router bearing, 1/2" I.D.	1
Bearing lock ring, 1/2" I.D.	1
24" brown steel standards	16
48" brown steel standards	8
Brown shelf clips (bags of 20)	3
Brown nails (bags of 50)	2
Mounting plates	4
Cup hinges	4
Speaker cloth (36" x 68")	1
1/4" shank rabbeting bit set (includes bearings for 5/16", 3/8", 7/16" and 1/2" rabbets)	1
23/32" mortising (plywood) bit,	1
Pattern flush-trim router bit, 3/4" diameter x 1-1/4" height, 1/2" shank	1
5/8" x 3/4" top-bearing mortise bit, 1/4" shank	1

*Available at woodworking stores and online.

The hardwood parts

With the cabinets together, you can cut and fit the other cabinet parts, such as adjustable shelves, drawer and door parts, and the plywood caps. Double-check to make sure the cut parts fit properly on the assembled bookcases.

Before you start cutting up the hardwood, sort through the boards. Set aside straight-grained pieces for door frames and face frames. On narrow parts, straight grain looks the best and is more stable. You may need to harvest the straight-grained edges from several boards to get the wood you want. For the doors, look for boards with straight grain that are free of warp. Also let them stabilize for a couple of days (Photo 8). For the face frames, a little warp is OK since the cabinets will hold them flat. The center cap uses wide stock, but in the end, the crown covers most of it and the upper face is above eye level. That means it's OK to use some less desirable wood with knots and other defects. Try to cut the drawer fronts from a single plank of wood so the grain matches.

Put it all together

Disassemble the cabinets and get ready for the big glue-up (Photo 10). For big jobs like this, use slow-setting glue. The extra 10 minutes of open time takes some of the pressure off complex glue-ups.

Assemble the bookcases and attach the face frames with glue. Rout and sand the face frames flush to the cabinet sides. Sand all unfinished parts to 180 grit.

Now you're ready to fit the cap parts and install the crown. First, you need to bolt the three cabinets together. If you don't have that kind of shop space, do one set at a time.

Align and mount the caps using countersunk screws to fasten them down. The caps have an even 3-in. overhang on the exposed sides of the cabinets. The caps on the side cabinets butt squarely into the side of the center cabinet.

Add lid stops along the bottom of the inside edge of the center cap. The stops will keep the lid from falling into the opening. Cut and fit the plywood lid for the top compartment. Mount the ring pull hardware to the lid.

Cut the crown molding (Photo 11). Give yourself extra length for test cuts. Add braces to your saw table to hold the crown in the same position as on the bookcase and to keep the molding from sliding as it's cut. Attach the crown with brad nails and molding glue. The heavy-bodied glue won't run or drip as you hold the crown in place for nailing. Sand the

crown smooth.

Cut the door parts to finished dimensions and assemble with biscuits. Rout a rabbet on the back of the opening. Use a wide chisel to square the inside corners. Drill holes for Euro hinges and mount the doors in the openings. Check for fit and even margins. Trim as necessary. Sand the door frames to 180 grit.

Assemble a 2x4 frame inside the TV opening. The setback of the frame depends on the depth of your TV and the mounting hardware you choose. Cover the frame with three panels. Use screws to fasten the middle panel. That makes it a removable access for wiring.

8 Air out your door parts. A couple of days of air circulation allows fresh-cut wood to stabilize. If any of the parts warp, you can cut new parts and avoid door warp after assembly.

CABLE NOTCH

BACKER BOARD

9 Gang-drill the vent holes. Stack up the shelves that will hold your electronics and tack them together with a couple of nails. Set a backer board under the stack to reduce blowout. Also cut notches for cords and cables.

CAUL

FACE FRAME

SHIM

10 Put it all together. Assemble in stages. Start with the plywood cabinet boxes. When the glue has dried, add the face frames. Use 2x4 "cauls" to apply even clamping pressure to the face frames.

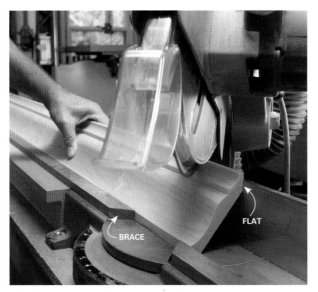

11 Brace the crown upside down. Position the crown molding with the bottom edge up. Add bracing to the saw's table to hold the crown at the correct angle. The flats on the back of the crown should sit flat against the fence and table.

12 Add speaker cloth to the doors. Pull the cloth tight across the opening and pin it into place with 1/4-in. x 1/4-in. cleats cut to fit the rabbet. Trim away the excess cloth with a utility razor blade.

Tips for keeping your electronics cool

Stay below 85 degrees

Studies show that for every 10-degree increase over 85 degrees, there's a 40 percent reduction in equipment life span.

To test your setup, place an electronic thermometer with a min/max function by each component. Check the temperature after a typical viewing session. If it's over 85 degrees, add ventilation.

Get the air moving

Air circulation is the key. You don't need powered fans to accomplish this unless the space is super-tight around your equipment. Our bookcase design creates a chimney effect where hot air is forced up and out of the cabinet as it draws cool air in through the speaker cloth in the doors.

Here are some tips to help create an effective airflow in your cabinet.
- Leave as much air space as possible between components; avoid packing them in tight.
- Place the hottest components on top so they can't bake the components above them. This also puts the hottest air nearest the exit. Big heat generators include cable boxes and powerful sound system amps. Cooler components include DVD/Blu-Ray players and lower-powered sound systems.
- Give each component its own shelf space.
- Vent the shelves. We drilled holes in our shelves.
- Enclosed TVs need at least a 1-in. gap all around.

Cut and fit the drawer fronts. Use shims to position the drawer fronts, then pin-nail them to the boxes. Next, pull the drawer out and clamp the front to the box for added security while drilling pilot holes from inside the box. Fasten the fronts with four No. 8 x 1-in. screws.

Finishing up

Remove the connector bolts and separate the cabinets. Remove the doors as well. Finish the bookcases with three coats of polyurethane. Give the interior its final coat when you brush on the exterior's third coat.

Mount the shelf standards. The standards have a numbering system to help in locating the clips. Be sure you mount the standards so the numbers rise as the standards run up the cabinet. Hold the nails with a needle-nose pliers to get them started

Take the finished doors and cut speaker cloth to fit over the opening with at least an inch of overhang. Press cherry cleats into place, pulling the cloth taut before you brad-nail the cleats into place (Photo 12).

Mounting your TV

TVs typically can use almost any mount, but be sure your set is not an exception. Check the owner's manual for specific mounting bracket recommendations. Be sure to buy a mounting bracket rated to hold the weight and dimension of your TV. Mount your TV so the screen is slightly behind the face frame. Avoid the tunnel effect caused by setting the TV too far back.

familyhandyman.com
- Want a foolproof formula for glass-smooth poly? Search for "polyurethane."
- Your router can do more jobs than you might think. Search for "router" to find out how.
- If you're not using pocket screw joinery, you're missing out. Search for "pocket screws" and get educated.

Cutting list

3/4" cherry plywood (5 sheets)

PART	QTY.	DIMENSIONS	NAME
A	2	13-1/4" x 85-1/4"	sides
B	4	13" x 47"	fixed shelves
C	3	12-1/2" x 19-1/8"	component shelves
D	2	12-1/2" x 25"	dividers; add 1/2" edge
E	3	15-1/2" x 33"	TV mount panels
F	4	9-1/4" x 77-3/4"	sides
G	6	9" x 29"	fixed shelves
H	10	7-1/2" x 28-3/8"	adjustable shelves; add 1-1/4" edges front/back
J	2	7" x 12-1/2"	drawer runners; add 1/2" edge
K	2	12-1/4" x 32-1/4"	cap; add 3/4" edges to front side
L	1	4" x 46-1/2"	toe board; add 1/2" on bottom edge
M	2	4" x 28-1/2"	toe board; add 1/2" on bottom edge
N	1	10" x 45"	lid; add 1/2" edging

1/4" cherry plywood (3 sheets)

PART	QTY.	DIMENSIONS	NAME
P	1	47-1/4" x 85-3/4"	back
Q	2	29-1/4" x 78-1/4"	backs

3/4" cherry hardwood

PART	QTY.	DIMENSIONS	NAME
R	2	2-1/2" x 85-1/4"	stiles; cut to 2-9/16" and trim flush to cabinet
S	4	2-1/2" x 77-3/4"	stiles; cut to 2-9/16" and trim flush to cabinet
T	1	3-1/2" x 43"	top rail
U	2	3-1/2" x 25"	top rails
V	3	1-1/2" x 43"	rails
W	4	1-1/2" x 25"	middle and bottom rails
X	1	4" x 54"	front of cap frame
Y	1	2" x 46"	back of cap frame
Z	2	4" x 17"	sides of cap frame
AA	20	1-1/4" x 28-3/8"	edging for adjustable shelf
BB	2	3/4" x 33"	front trim on cap
CC	2	3/4" x 13"	side trim on cap
DD	3	3/4" x 19-1/8"	component shelf trim
EE	3	7-1/4" x 7-3/4"	drawer fronts
FF	4	2" x 23-3/4"	door stiles
GG	2	2-1/2" x 13-7/8"	bottom door rail
HH	2	2" x 13-7/8"	top door rail

1/2" cherry hardwood

PART	QTY.	DIMENSIONS	NAME
JJ	6	2-1/2" x 5"	plinth blocks
KK	2	3/4" x 25"	divider edge
LL	3	3/4" x 6-1/2"	drawer runner edge
MM	2	3/4" x 13-1/4"	skid
NN	4	3/4" x 9-1/4"	skid
PP	2	3/4" x 46"	lid trim
QQ	2	3/4" x 10"	lid trim

Crown molding

PART	QTY.	DIMENSIONS	NAME
RR	1	4" x 18'	cut to length for front and sides

1/2" Baltic birch plywood

PART	QTY.	DIMENSIONS	NAME
SS	6	7-3/8" x 12-1/2"	drawer sides
TT	3	7-3/8" x 6"	drawer fronts
UU	3	6-7/8" x 6"	drawer backs

1/4" Baltic birch plywood (could use leftover cherry plywood)

PART	QTY.	DIMENSIONS	NAME
VV	3	5-15/16" x 12"	drawer bottoms

Figure B Dado layout

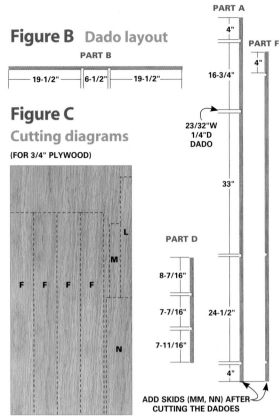

Figure C
Cutting diagrams
(FOR 3/4" PLYWOOD)

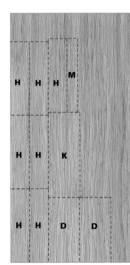

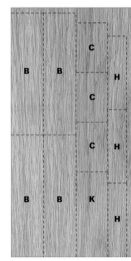

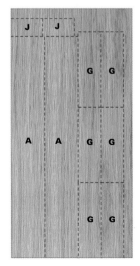